Spun Yarns and Woven Words

Edited by Mary Farrell

North Coast Writers

Graphic content and motifs designed by Sinead Coxhill, Mae Gardiner, Paul Girvan, Helen Hand and Janet Peace.

ISBN: 978-1-915819-16-1

OTHER TITLES BY IMPSPIRED

Daddy's girl –
by Isabelle Cory

Tobias -
By Mark Pearce

Fetch –
By Yvonne Hamilton

Adele & Tom –
By Chella Courington

Periodic Stories Vol.4 –
By Jim Bates

Happy Endings –
By Charlie Zamarripa

Echoes –
By Gordon Ferris

IMPSPIRED

10% of all proceeds from this Anthology

will go to

two Charities

* * * * *

Macmillan Cancer Support

The Samaritans

Contents

Paul Girvan

Yvonne Hamilton

Helen Hand

Brendan Magee

Acknowledgements of First Publication

Robin Holmes

Bluebell was published in *Heartland,* a CAP Anthology, 2021.
As if was shortlisted for the *Eighth Annual Bangor Poetry Competition* & published in December 2020.
Knitting was shortlisted for the *Sixth Annual Bangor Competition* & published in September 2018.

Geraldine Fleming

Cartographer by Geraldine Fleming was published in *Threshold,* a CAP Anthology, 2022.
Undeserving by Geraldine Fleming was published in *Curiosity, Impspired Press, January 2023.*
Sunday Lunch by Geraldine Fleming was published in *Impspired Magazine,* 1st June 2021.
Noble Moments by Geraldine Fleming was published in *Crow of Minerva Journal,* 16th April 2021.
Hidden in Plain Sight by Geraldine Fleming was published in *Curiosity, Impspired Press, January 2023.*

Sinead Coxhill

The Magic Box was published in the online magazine *sagecigarettes.com,* 2022.

Yvonne Hamilton

Roy was published in *Fetch, A Canine Collection,* by Yvonne Hamilton, published by *Impspired Press, 2023.*
The Last Dance was first published in *Love, Loss and Cardiac Issues, Impspired, 2022.*

Helen Hand

Peru, 1980 was published in *Love, Loss and Cardiac Issues,* Impspired Press, 2022.
The Loch (formerly *Remembering)* and *Molly and Ted* were published in *Pen to Paper,* compiled by Lucan Creative Writers Group, published by 5 to 50 Books, 2015.
Window on Beara was shortlisted for the *The Jonathan Swift Creative Writers Awards,* held in Dublin, 2022.

Brenda McAteer

Thirteen Seconds was published in the Anthology *Love, Loss and Cardiac Issues,* Impspired Press 2022.

Orla McFaul

Our Wish For You was written for, and read at, a Wedding Mass, April 2022.

Janet Peace

Tapestry has been published in the Anthology *Love, Loss and Cardiac Issues,* and in *Springboards: a Manual of Creative Writing,* both published by Impspired Press in 2022.

Sue Steging

a naming of parts, longlisted for the Seamus Heaney Award for New Writing, was published in the CAP Anthology *Threshold,* 2022. *bonfire* was published in the CAP Anthology *Heartland* 2021. *At Knockoneill Court Tomb* was published in *The Bangor Literary Journal, Issue 18,* September 2022.

Rhona Stephens

Greeting was published in the Anthology *Love, Loss and Cardiac Issues,* Impspired Press 2022.

Mary Farrell

Hearth Matters appeared in the Anthology *Love, Loss and Cardiac Issues* published by Impspired Press, 2022.

Introduction
By Rhona Stephens

Welcome to Spun Tales and Woven Words, the second anthology from North Coast Writers. Readers who enjoyed our first collection will be pleased to see familiar names among the contributors, but there are fresh voices too, from talented writers who have joined our circle more recently. Together, we have woven truth and tall tales to produce an anthology we hope you will enjoy.

Strands of connection and contrast thread their way through these poems and short stories. There are fragrant roses, bluebells and camomile lawns, ice creams and ice skates, wry rural tales and travelogues. Some pieces will make you smile, others make you weep. A few will make you laugh out loud. You will find wit and whimsy, tales of love and loss, pieces that roll along at a cracking pace and poignant moments over which you will linger.

So choose a quiet space, turn the page and allow us to take you on a journey from the salty waters of Ireland's north coast across the wild Atlantic to Peru, by magic carpet to Samarkand, to Venice, and home again via Beara on Ireland's southwestern shores.

Robin Holmes

To everything there is a season

Growing up on a small hill farm in the Mourne Mountains in Northern Ireland for Robin was a deeply formative experience for his writing. In his poetry he explores themes of the natural world, the life of birds, the changing seasons and man's problematic relationship to the environment. His work has appeared regularly in the Bangor Literary Journal published online, and the annual CAP Poetry in Motion Journals published in Northern Ireland.

Bluebells

You will find them, deep in untrodden sunglades,
murmurings of bluebells, marvellous,
mesmerised in their own melancholy;
waving trumpet, trinket bell heads,
each a phial of lapus lazuli,
azure alchemy of blue blended
sea mist and sky scrapings.

Between tree trunks, they occupy with temerity
the rutted, corrugated earth,
glowing in glaucous gaze,
merging into becalmed lagoons.
Imbibe their scent, delicate, diaphanous
as a gauze of gossamer, reviving
the tiredest soul, the dankest lungs.

Charmed out of chilled soil by the leitmotif of
resurgent thrushes, ebullient blackbirds,
from dawn to dusk they surge
under a pebble-dashed wall of sound;
miniature mirrors,
capturing, reflecting
the blue vaulted sky.

Yet tread carefully, as if on holy ground,
soon this shall be the graveyard of beauty.
These glistening sapphires will lose their sheen,
shrivel and shrink into a bulbous underground,
a dessicated dreamland. The year marches on,
some gawdy impostor awaits in the wings,
ready to enthral the wayward traveller.

As if
(A Reflection on Whin Blossom)

As if
an opportunist thief sneaked up
on the sleeping mid-day sun,
then stole his yellow cardigan,
snipped it with scissors,
unravelled all that golden wool,
before embroidering it into all
of the hedgerows and ditches
of Ireland.

As if
a deranged alchemist
devised a new recipe,
collected tons of daffodils,
primroses, buttercups,
dandelions and strained egg yolk,
pouring it into huge vats,
where it boiled and simmered
for days, before spraying it onto
all the hedgerows and ditches
of Ireland

As if
I travelled back in time
to a street in Arles
a night café, a bad house
perhaps, and rescued Vincent
from a bottle of absinthe,
an argument with Gaugain
over a skinny woman.
'Come', I said, 'back to Ireland,
bring tubes of burnt umber,
cadmium yellow, come and paint
our hedgerows, our ditches
give them the immortality
you have bestowed on
sunflowers, wheatfields, gleaners.
There will be no crows,
no threatening skies.'
So he came and painted
all the hedgerows and ditches
of Ireland.

Knitting

In your cupboard, amidst
the acquired detritus of ninety years,
a ball of wool, navy blue and
starling speckled.
A Valentine's heart
pierced by two needles.
Each evening,
after a frugal tea,
you sat, with a widow's silence
knitting stitches, casting on,
knitting stitches, casting on,
knitting stitches, casting on,
the snick of needles,
regular as a loom.
Your hands then,
arthritic, hacked and calloused,
yet each pendulum evening
was measured out by inches,
until a lengthening
snake of a scarf touched the floor.
You produced scarves
for those you loved;
distributing them, as if
The Queen, on a Maundy Thursday,
until one evening
you put the wool down, forever
When was that?

Your mind seemed to enter a tunnel,
dense with mist, with fog.
Your life got stuck
in reverse gear.
We heard the rasping of clutch plates
and feared, as your coordination collapsed;
the slow disintegration
of an ordered world.
And so you spent
the next decade
knitting memories,
giving us sepia toned scarf stories
to keep the cold away.

So we meet again my heartache

~ after Melody Gardot ~

So we meet again my heartache,
at this table set for two.
The *À La Carte,* for broken hearts,
the Specials, all prepared by you.

So we meet again my heartache,
each restless night I toss and turn.
No blissful sleep, no kisses deep,
how you prolong my dark sojourn.

So we meet again my heartache,
with memories which sear me through.
The dagger glides, with words inscribed
'I once loved you.'

So we meet again my heartache,
is there no place I can go?
My grief is stretched, in black fishnets,
one mawkish last tango.

And so we meet again my heartache,
like some black raven from above.
Here to haunt me, still you taunt me.
then dance me to the end of love.

A Trespass

I knew I was trespassing from the start; the sense of violation, an intrusion, the moving through a portal into a forbidden world, the past prised open like an oyster shell. At first the old door resisted, swollen and tight but with my shoulder against it and all my strength, it gave way. It was almost an eerie sound, the rasping of wood across stone, the loosening of time's clenched fist, until finally a narrow gap into which I was able to fit and then slip through, silent as a letter through a post box.

Immediately the door opened into a living room buttered thick with dust, soot, mildew and spider webs; the detritus of decay. As ever, the larger symbols of domesticity lay as scattered chess pieces across the room; a table, four chairs, two armchairs and a settee punctured with springs, now looking like cold metallic mushrooms, denying any comfort. On the mantlepiece, often the central altar of rural dwellings, a rusting tin of Andrews Liver Salts and an ancient bottle with the label still intact, 'Veno's Cough Mixture'.

At first I felt as if I was in a kind of antique shop heaven, but the realization soon set in that this was a haunted pharmacy. Such medication only hobbled the irresistible lava flow of mortality. The once inhabitants of this time capsule were long since dead. I was raking about in their crypt. Or was I? I noticed a pile of old magazines and newspapers lying on a small table. At last something to place the dwelling firmly in a point in space and time; a chance to get coordinates to the real outside world. I picked up a dusty magazine merely titled 'ILLUSTRATED - 4D Every Wednesday', amazingly dated August 27th, 1955.

My fascination burning, I proceeded up the stairs slowly, perilously, as a corkscrew. I had a vision of the wood cracking beneath my feet and my body dropping as if through an invisible trap door. Yet the rotten steps held me as I grasped the banister for added security, as a blind man might do. In a desolate bedroom a metallic bedstead resembled a mangled torture rack, partially covered in a grey blanket. I lifted it up to reveal a hostel for sleeping spiders. The sense of decay was oppressive, ghastly and searing. Any pattern on the faded wallpaper was so ancient it resembled a cave drawing.

Then it happened! I was a burglar alarm to the silent sentinel of this deserted turret. Flying towards me, like a screeching Stuka, was a Peregrine fledgling, sickle beaked and claws dangling like barbed wire. He seemed to be trying to land on my head, attacking me with the fury of a demon. This feathered landlord's eviction was ruthless and instantaneous. I dropped like a pinball down the helter-skelter of the stairs, through the door and back out into the safety of the silent world I never should have left. I turned my back on the tainted, haunted ruin, a tuber to the high priests of decay.

It was only when I got back into my car five minutes later that I realized I had rolled up that magazine and stuffed it into a deep pocket. If I calmed down should I take it back and leave it where I found it? No, I didn't deliberate for too long on that possibility, but just wanted to get away as fast as possible. I imagine the Atlantic's twin spears of wind and rain have now obliterated that ancient dwelling.

As for my trespass, it remains unforgiven.

Geraldine Fleming

Geraldine Fleming retired early due to ill health. Drawn back into creative writing she found a supportive community when she joined North Coast Writers Group in Northern Ireland. She enjoys writing both poetry and prose and has published in a number of journals, magazines and anthologies. She loves to write. Most recently, in 2022, two poems were published in *Threshold, the CAP Anthology,* and her poem *Cartographer* was long listed for the *Seamus Heaney Award. Also in 2022, her* short stories appeared in two new anthologies, *Love, Loss and Cardiac Issues, Impspired Press* and *New Worlds: New Voices, Ulster University Press.* Her debut short story collection, *Curiosity,* was released in January 2023 by *Impspired Press.*

Cartographer

you started with stubby wax crayons
rubbed on smoothed-out brown paper
X marked the spot amid spur-heavy palm trees
your first treasure map fades in a forgotten box

~

long slim drawers house flat-world images
scratched on clay tablets
drawn on vellum
printed on grades of paper
swathes of triangulated surveys
measured by human hand
scanned by satellite
transposed as oceans and continents
with rivers and mountains
deserts and jungles
borders and blocks
perpetual fine-tuning for fidelity

~

scale models determined by history
land-wars and sea battles
navigating conquest routes
spice routes
slave routes
extinction routes

~

on the near-time horizon you see
coastlines crash and melt into
rising oceans of human carelessness
terra firma shrinks beyond redress
climates pivot while populations plummet
wringing your hands
your mercurial map wears thin

Undeserving

The penetrating alarm failed to drag her from sleep, from the void of her late-night medication cocktail. Her breathing was shallow, eyelids shielding her from another nightmare. Consciousness struggled, bobbing in the opioid sea she fed herself nightly. Then she heard him, beyond her alarm, beyond the miasma.

'Mum, Mum, time for brekkie, time to get up.'

The light chimes of her son's voice provided an antidote of adrenaline. Her hammering heart and rushing blood forced her fogbound mind to form the thought, to trigger the movement.

Cathy stood up, an inherent parental response. She dumped the alarm and arranged herself like a new-strung puppet ready to take her first step.

'Coming Ettie, my sweet-pea. What do you fancy for breakfast?'

She pulled her bedraggled brown hair into a knot as she made her way to the kitchen, oblivious to the debris of her unattended home. Ettie was not in his usual seat at the table. He was not swinging his tanned legs, stretched by a recent growth spurt, singing to himself.

'Oh Ettie, so it's hide and seek this morning. OK, ready or not.'

The unfamiliar crease of a smile replaced her ingrained grimace.

'Bet you're in the garden. I'm coming to find you.'

Echoes of her playful lilt broke the silence as she leaned over the kitchen sink to check the garden. Not for the first time, the stinking dishes rearranged themselves. From the corner of her eye, she fancied she caught Ettie's heel nip into his bedroom.

She beelined there next. Empty. The spotless, cosy room, was estranged from the rest of the house. A neat bed, an abundance of shelved toys and knick-knacks betrayed its status. Reality crashed in, driving a distraught Cathy into the bathroom.

She buckled to the floor at the sight of the Kl'qui drug caddy perched like a homing beacon on the side of the sink. Opened only by her fingerprint, it released to her touch. Her breath was ragged and the prism of tears diffused the jewel-coloured pills. Something to help no matter how you felt, or didn't want to feel. Clicking out two citrine pills she swallowed them dry and waited for the initial wash of calm. A crutch to cope with melancholia, a treasure chest of numbness and if you chose, finality. The Kl'qui were not unsympathetic. The golden triquetral insignia taunted her, forcing her to remember. She tried focusing on the lines of the ceramic floor, she knew they scored straight across in squares, but not yet. Pressing herself against the tiles she swiped waves of despair from mid-air replays.

Reliving gatherings of families and friends, bubbling with excitement, eager to receive the wisdom of an advanced culture, humanity's benefactors. Six months after first contact the Kl'qui visitors spoke to the world, global media was awash with speculation. How would the visitors introduce them to the other races, how would they share their technology and enable advancement. So many possibilities, so many futures, galaxies to explore. The visitor's technology enriched the human race's understanding of the universe, reinventing their understanding of existence, of sentience. Even those inclined towards conspiracies were hopeful in their speculations.

The Kl'qui assessment of the planet changed everything. The message was short and ice-cold, humans were undeserving of their world and thereby undeserving of the children of Earth. She shivered and shrivelled away from the memory, optimism and hope turned to shock and despair. That was the moment, in her opinion, the world plunged into dark chaos. Earth's representatives tried to engage again and again, tried to negotiate the children's' return, everyone held their breath, hoping and praying, The Kl'qui's motives were inscrutable. Global impotence spawned world-wide melancholia. So many friends gave up hope within the first few months. She had attended funerals almost daily, the grief of their loss robbing them of life.

Each day began the same for Cathy. First the density of denial, then an assisted struggle to function in the new reality. She managed to stand up. After the medication she was always gripped by a fierce thirst, she drank from the faucet. Barely recognising her image in the mirror, she moved her lips, thin and blue. Her words unsynchronised, like some badly dubbed actor. She ran her trembling hands over her face, digging palms into her eyes.

'I don't know you. What the hell happened you?'

Hollow-eyes, waxen face, hunched shoulders and aged beyond her forty years she began her ritual of recovery and reinstatement, raising cupped hands of water to her face. She only wished she could say it felt good. Nothing had felt right since she lost Ettie. All the Earth's children were gone, four years now and no children had been born. Fetuses disappeared from wombs and no one could conceive. One day the children were there the next everyone under sixteen was gone. Ettie would be ten.

Within thirty minutes she had showered and finished her first coffee of the day. She perched the fusty cup back on the crockery mountain. Allowing herself to blind-eye the family photo, she pushed on with her routine.

Her husband, Finn had left. He accepted the Kl'qui's resettlement offer and left for some new world. She had watched the armada leave orbit two years ago. They left their home planet on a trail of lost dreams and fractured futures. There had been no contact from the leavers, the armada had gone silent. Cathy knew she would never see Finn again. She chose to remain at home, hoping the children would be returned. The photo framed the world of her loss.

Cathy lifted her uniform from the back of the bedroom door. Now dressed she returned to the bathroom mirror, checked her reflection again. She adjusted her shirt, straightened her jacket, recaptured a strand of hair and took the remainder of her medication. Just enough to get her through another day.

She retrieved her revolver from the safe and holstered it. Pocketed her police identification and clipped on her radio as she walked out the door ready for work. Cathy understood the Kl'qui valued dedication. Humanity's last glowing ember of hope depended on the recovery of an abused world.

Sunday Lunch

the last gravy you ever made
meaty fat and onion sweet
sheened by a dashing butter ball
chemistry in motion

cornflour speckles moonscapes the pan lid
leftover evidence in subdued focus
selenology mapping ash cones and rilles

stove clouds belch from
your garden's root crop
condensing on the cool wall
meteorology experiment epitomised

butter lava flowing over skin split potatoes
slow moving down the starch mountain
volcanology delight

Bramleys laid in beds of rich pastry
glee filled with anticipation
alchemy demystified

noble moments

an ancient goldsmith traces
daring veins back to the treasures of Varna
crafting at his ease-curved bench
earnestly focused
this artisan in aurum
bends and shapes
with fire and mettle
tap/ drill/ saw/ file
experience cast in solid forms

a timeline of hallmarked headlines

as lemel cradles in the drape of the bench skin
modest remains from noble endeavours
slivers of shards
flecks of flakes
grains of goldust
so capsule moments are ignored until
memories are revalued

Hidden in Plain Sight

Erin lifted the mail from the sand-trap mat. Two brown envelopes.

'Bill and bill,' she tossed them on the hall table.

The third was not a bill. It was handwritten, a flourish of loops on a stiff white envelope. Her name, *Erin Littlewood,* sheepishly waited for her to notice it. Turning the envelope over and back she watched tiny lights dance across the pearlized surface. Flicking the back of the envelope she recalled seven cards last Christmas and four text messages on her birthday. Her circle of contacts had admittedly diminished. She bit her lip focusing her powers of deduction on the card, pivoting it between her fingers. It refused to give away any secrets. The script was unfamiliar and she could not think of any significant events coming up. The only thing to do, if she wanted to know who had sent it and what it was about was open the card. She tapped the envelope against her lower lip. With a decisive twist of her wrist, she propped it on the table.

'Later' she nodded at the white wrapped puzzle.

Picking up Raggles' lead was like the first tap of a conductor's baton. He was ready to play, his excitement bubbled, nearing chaos. Twice daily with the turn of the tide they trekked along the beach. Tide out, coat on, her rescue collie tugging eager on his well-stretched lead.

'If we delay another second, you will surely combust. Can't have that now, can we? Come on, good boy.'

He calmed just enough for her to clip the lead onto his collar. As ever the thunk of the closing door echoed, intense and hollow, incongruous in her small bungalow. No matter how abundant her soft furnishings and deep pile rugs, the sound of desolation was deep-rooted, inescapable. Its sonic imprint lingered. This stinging reminder filled a place he had never lived. The walls had never chimed with his deep tones, his *enjoy your walk* chuckle had never rippled these walls.

***

Close readings of police reports and visits to the accident site had only intensified her confusion. She felt simultaneously mired in despair and dislocated from her own psyche. Without him she existed, just existed. She knew he would never have wanted to leave her, not like this. Frozen in shock, suspended between a world she refused to accept and a world she could never restore, she sought answers in floating feathers and fence-hopping Robins. Searching his pockets and flipping through the pages of his books for some sign, some note, some secret message from him became a regular obsession. TV channels and radio stations were changed to map his habits, surely, he was reaching out – his favourite programme or piece of music could be significant.

'I just need to know where to look. Please, please... help me find a sign you are with me... Please.'

Invariably she found herself sitting in the midst of mayhem trying to create order, an order that she could accept. Each evening she watched shadows grow in the darkness of their bedroom. It felt like trying to interpret long ago cast runes or read faceless tarot cards.

***

Erin returned to work urged by relatives who hoped that routine would help her breathe a bit easier. Her colleagues in biostatistics welcomed her back. After all, she was the Research Lead with years of experience. She had mentored most of the team. Everyone was shocked when they saw her. Myrtle on reception, the weathervane of the team, reflected their concerns in the tea room.

'She just isn't herself, how could you expect her to be? She's obviously not eating, she's skin and bone. Not sleeping either I'd say. She won't let herself grieve- pure shock, I'm sure.'

Something vital had changed in Erin. She pursued patterns that could not possibly exist either in the data or in life. Sifting for correlations that fell outside research, beyond the bounds of science. By the end of the third week, she found herself still in her pyjamas scrutinising the texture on her breakfast toast at three o'clock one Friday afternoon. It was then she acknowledged that the sharp edge of the mental axe had separated her from her understanding of the world. Conrad's words returned to her time and again.

You, my darling can solve anything, you are my Solutionist.

She decided to retire.

***

After the second anniversary she recognised that her grief had exhausted family and friends. Those once supportive visits dwindled in frequency. Life in the city screamed infinite reminders of the cosmic shift, suffocating her. She imagined how concerns transmuted into relief when she decided to move nearer the sea. A seeker only seeking confirmation, or at least reassurance. Of what though, she really was not sure. Meaning and purpose and connectedness had left like morning mist carried on a last breath. On his last breath.

Looking back, Erin understood that the search had started after Conrad died, after the police had knocked the door, after his ashes were handed to her, after sympathies and explanations caught her in a web of inertia.

The first summer in the bungalow she had walked her stretch of beach in sandals. Curving along the dampened sand line, the granulated pulp squeezing between tanned toes bound in blue straps. The rasp of wet grains reminding her about touch. Ozone forced her to breathe, forced her to remember, charging her with energy she didn't want. The shifting character of the shore and dunes, sky and sea, a constant message - everything changes. Change she rejected.

Each time she tried to retrace her exact steps her path had been subsumed by nature's vigour. Pressing each foot precisely on the sand, right foot forward heel to toe, shifting her weight from her left sandal to the right, then repeat. Her imprint reclaimed each time. Like a ghost walking through this new life. Each outing in her sandals reminded her of Balos in Crete, their last holiday. There they had matched each other's stride for stride, hand in hand, too absorbed to notice their footprints didn't last there either. Perhaps there it didn't matter.

***

Now summer was a few turned pages on her calendar and autumn was succumbing to winter. As she strode out, her stout boots left a fading impression along the beach. The daily analysis continued with each morning walk. Clouds and contrails were scrutinised and dismissed, the froth of receding tide and the tangle of seaweeds were all given due consideration. She couldn't contemplate missing a sign, a signal, blinking at the wrong moment could be disastrous. The search for meaning permeated every aspect of her life.

Raggles' barking wrenched her back from her impromptu reverie. Her focus had wavered and she never wavered. She retrieved a whipping strand of brown hair and pushed it under her woolly hat. Raggles ran round her in semicircles herding her, his tail low, his eyes intent on bending her to his will. Erin moved obediently, curious to see what this display was all about. He came to rest near the dunes, a paw either side a half-buried shell.

'Well, boy, what have you found here? What is so important?

Erin bent down to ruffle his fur, usually a game changer for him. Not this time though, he continued to nose the shell, quite unlike a collie, unlike Raggles. Without thinking she hunkered down to lever the shell from the wind-dried sand.

Bigger than it seemed, about the size of the palm of her hand. No razored edges or fatal flaws. She turned it over and back. It was the cup side of a scallop shell. Shaded ridges fanned out from the fractured hinge moving from earthy tones to flecks of flamingo pink. Inside it was smooth, fringed with grey and a perfect iridescent white begging to be touched. Cold finger tips traced along the stria. Only half of what it once was, yet still whole, still complete.

Raggles waited with unusual patience as she manoeuvred the shell through every angle. No one else witnessed it, but as Erin raised her eyes to the far horizon, she knew she had found her lens. The long-clouded perspective dispersed. Not by a message, but something far simpler. A random element in all the hunted signs finally triggered her acceptance of her grief. Her solution. There was no missed pattern, no moment she had overlooked.

Like the half-buried shell, she was still whole. Conrad existed in her, in her memories, in each heartbeat and always would. She wiped her tears, her first tears from her pale blue eyes since Conrad died. Knocking the last few grains of sand from the shell she tucked it into her pocket. Turning into the wind they headed for home. Each step gaining renewed purpose. Her tears were there now, her grief was surfacing. The white envelope would be opened, the invitation accepted and she would make some long overdue calls. The scourge of the impossible search was relegated to the past.

Sinead Coxhill

Living in Northern Ireland in the beautiful north coast town of Portrush, Sinead's poetry is often inspired by the sea and coastal landscape. In 2019 she performed at the Red Sails and Stendhal Festivals in Northern Ireland and in the same year toured England performing at various Open Mic events and Waterstones in Birmingham. Her poems have been published in *Spindrift, 2018* & *Reeling In, 2021,* two anthologies by Portrush Writers. Her work can also be seen in *Heartland,* the CAP anthology 2020, and in *Irish Hares and Seahorses,* a North Coast Writers anthology and *Love, Loss and Cardiac Issues* both published by Impspired.com in 2022. Also in 2022, she had work published in *Across the Threshold,* a pamphlet and companion publication to CAP's *Threshold* anthology, and in the online magazine, *sagecigarettes.com.*

Today I Miss the Sea

today I miss the sea
too cold and squally
to brave the walk
in parka and boots
squeamish   sequestered
snuggled in the warmth
made soft by the smiling weather
of the last two weeks

today I miss the sea
and wonder how she seems

is she hurling herself violently
against the sea wall

or is she coyly calm
only slightly ruffled by the wind

today I miss the sea

Murmuration

silver scintillating sea
like poured solder

I think of the word
murmuration

it perfectly describes
the music of gentle waves

it's decided
it's been re-invented

Incantation

you were the first person I told

telephone shrinking the

hundreds of miles

told you how that boy

inside me was gone

came too early to survive

you kept repeating

poor girl *poor girl*

like a sorrowful incantation

somehow sound soothed me

enabled the telling of my story

without breaking down

The Magic Box

~ after Kit Wright ~

I will put in the box…
footfalls of angels
tinkling laughter of children
soft strumming of a harp

I will put in the box…
joyful sound of a yodel
leap of a small ballet dancer
fog that rolls across a river

I will put in the box…
ice maiden dancing in the sun
frown of an old curmudgeon
mermaid wearing a red jumper

I will put in the box…
icy splash of sea on my skin
salmon swimming in honey
mackerel dancing a jig

my box is made from scales shed by snakes
shimmering pink   green   gold
its handles are jewelled   ancient crab claws

I shall carry my box with care
aboard a sailing ship with a bright green sail
we shall navigate the briny ocean
gliding into a sunset

The Elf on the Shelf

The berries on the holly wreath were wizened, the leaves brown and crunchy. Unhooked from the front door it went into the compost bin.

Decorations taken down, faded areas of paintwork were revealed. Carrie folded away the artificial tree. Baubles, strings of shining tinsel and fairy lights were packed. It brought a lump to her throat to see the house, it seemed lonely, forlorn and abandoned.

Just one decoration left. Seated on the mantelpiece was the elf. He was clad entirely in red – tunic, tights and lace trimmed cap, his slim legs dangling, his feet in wooden clogs.

She thought of leaving him there for company, but worried it might be unlucky, so he too was packed away. It felt like losing a friend.

The elf lay flat in the cardboard box, claustrophobic in the darkness. He didn't relish the prospect of being confined for another year.

He remembered with fondness his place on the mantelpiece. The woman wrote stories and poetry, and he could listen as she read her work aloud. *How to get out of this prison?* Raising his legs, he pushed the lid of the box with his feet, but, felt only the tiniest movement. He kept going until tired and shaky.

The lead soldiers had watched his struggle. The captain called them to attention and they formulated an escape plan for the elf. It was agreed that two of the most athletic soldiers would act as a climbing frame. Another would give the elf a leg up until he stood with a foot on each man's shoulder.

The plan was speedily executed. The elf, now much closer to the lid, could push with his shoulders and hands. Soon he had succeeded in pushing it clear and scrambling down the side, called a cheery *Thank you* to his helpers. Once outside his normal powers were restored and he wasted no time in flying to the living room.

Resuming his position, he crossed his legs. When Carrie came downstairs next morning she saw him straight away.

Startled she mused, "I could have sworn I'd packed you away."

Reaching out to pick him up, she noticed his crossed legs.

Your legs were definitely dangling before.

He winked at her from his black right eye. She shook her head in disbelief, so he winked at her again. She laughed.

I think you're my lucky elf. You can stay.

Mae Gardiner

Living on the North Coast of Ireland, Mae Gardiner draws inspiration from the people and places around her. She writes children's fairy tales, poetry, short stories and also paints. Having performed at Atlantic Craft NI Events throughout Ireland, her *'A Coat of Many Colours'*, 2020, is available on YouTube . Many of her poems were first published in three Anthologies from Portrush Writers Group, *Beachcombing* 2014, *Spindrift* 2018 and *Reeling In* 2021. Three of her pieces featured in the Anthology from North Coast Writers, *Irish Hares and Seahorses,* and her poem *Not just yet* featured in the Anthology *Love, Loss and Cardiac Issues,* both of which were published by Impspired Press in 2022.

empty vessel

her face tilts
towards sunbeams
grateful for evening rays

boats chug into harbour
their catch safe & crowning
in the womb below decks

her womb worthless
an empty cargo
deserted   desolate   dry

she remembers fondly
times of fullness & creation
a belly-filled hull

now a wasted vessel
battered by hormonal storms
jealous of abilities

to birth
ideas
children

in another cycle
the moon still
ebbs and flows

time marches on
looks over his shoulder
mocking

Untitled Love

the beginning was like a tidal wave   a storm
I quenched your thirst
never tiring

I was seen felt heard loved
I gave
myself   all   everything

now broken
time   years understanding
I want to be back where the river flows
side by side with your love

a chasm appeared overnight
and a waterfall pumps
downwards   out the pipe
nothing left but a drip

reaching out
my parched lips   those same lips
you no longer touch
sometimes   finding
a puddle
of love   but
it's murky
with change uncertainty decisions

you remain
complicated complex continuous
you flow away from me
and leave me
in drought

Unforeseen

followed by the Moon

in a Saturn cycle

baptized by Mars

fire and water

he rose powerful

like the phoenix

gathered the strength

of a storm

and clinging tight

became the wind

THE KEENING TREE

The pine tree was standing keening at the foot of the stairs, and so it should

That tree deserved never to be happy again, it should suffer the consequences of its joviality … but not today

It could lie and rot beside the black bin until summer came, it could starve there for all she cared

She had returned for a different purpose – to try and stop something happening which would leave a torn fragment in her heart forever

Her intention was to embroider pieces of "what ifs", some "I should have dones" and cobble a single "I wish I could turn the clock back" into its branches

The pure white walls stood glumly behind the tree

"Tree, you should be ashamed," she said out loud believing the walls might blush and turn away

Paul Girvan

We are the bees of the invisible

A recent member of North Coast Writers, as a senior barrister and then as a judge Paul Girvan wrote extensively on legal matters during a long career. He now enjoys the freedom of creative writing particularly poetry which is often inspired by his travels, by nature and by his sense of place, history and time. A keen amateur artist his work is influenced by an artist's eye for colour, form and atmosphere. In 2022 Paul contributed to the Anthology *Love, Loss and Cardiac Issues* and in 2023 to Issue 21 of the online magazine and the printed version thereof all published by Impspired Press.

Florentine Dawn

Red Medici ball, the sun upslips, upslides,
back lights in pink etched churches' domes
palazzo walls, suffused in light, now echoing
not yet the sounds of tramping tourist feet
but sounds of armoured ghosts, the clash of arms,
the rustling of Renaissance silks, unsheathing swords,
dark whispering condottieri, mad Pazzi
lusting for blood to spill on duomo's floor

while in Giotto's tower the campanone tolls.

In market, sun uplit, a jumble of empty boxes,
evokes that smoking, bonfired pile of vanities;
accursèd Savonarol' dark cursing still
as cynic serpent Machiavel' drips poison
into the ears of dukes, princes, prelates;
fat, flatulent Leo, the butt of Luther's wrath,
bestrides his horse along the muddy Arno's banks
while coins of gold tinkle into banker's hands

while in Giotto's tower the campanone tolls.

Still climbs the sun seeking its zenith
building its furnace heat and wilting
the drummed-out whispers from the past,
those sounds of tramping tourist feet
sun stripping the ancient peeling paint
sun melting the old-time jingling coins
sun burning up the ancient vanities
yet past is present - it is not gone

still in Giotto's tower the campanone tolls.

In the Garden of Good and Evil

Two arms embrace two lakes   turquoise on silk
Belpaese's true delight that garden paradise
where sun flung diamonds gleam and glint
Lecco Lake and Como shimmer join and meld
where once Bethrothed there walked and kissed
Rodrigo's evil clutches fled   that devil Don
here blue waters lick and gentle lap serene
the Villa Monastero's slopes all verdant green.

I came with easel brush and paints to stand
imbibe the Alps majestic soaring magic grand
see plants arrayed in coloured serried banks
jag leaved upstretching shrubs soft leavèd trees
quivering in that italic balmy passing breeze
a convent garden once it was now long displaced
expelled those fallen sisters lustful lewd disgraced
by lives of broken vows and lies exiled erased.

As there I quiet watched and drank all deeply in
came rustle from a shaded spine leaved pine
long languorous slithering slimy green it slid
a snake that stopped and greedy eyed its prey
it raised its head grew still and cold eyed stared
then fork tongued struck and sated belly crawled
back through dead and dusty crackling leaves.
Spell broken Paradise re-lost old Eden's tale reprised.

Note

The Villa Monastero is one of the loveliest gardens in Italy a country which the Italians rightly call il Belpaese the beautiful land. It overlooks the confluence of Lakes Como and Lecco. In the 16th century it was the site of a nunnery closed down by Papal Bull because of the debauched lives of the nuns. Subsequently the property passed in the hands of a family into which the sister of Alessandro Manzoni married. Manzoni's set his great novel The Betrothed in this region of Italy. It is the tale of two young lovers Lucia and Renzo whose marriage the evil Don Rodrigo set out to prevent.

Samarkand

Not borne by djinnis on a Persian silken rug
we arrived on a train, a trundling train,
that shook its way across the Central Asian wastes
from Turkman Ashgabat, weird marble city,
figment of a despot's mind, yet realised,
white tombstone blocks, empty of souls.
The omnipresent president stares down
while cuddly laughing dogs he strokes.

We cross dull desiccated desert lands,
the untold wealth the oils and gas beneath
into Uzbeks' empty lands- more limbo sands,
punctuated by madrassas, mosques, minarets,
tiled turquoise, cobalt blue and emerald green,
shimmering invitations to the Paradise beyond.
Bukhara and Khiva, harems, pools, slave markets
echoing still to the sound of murderous lash.

To Samarkand, the jewel box of Tamerlane,
Temur the Lame lying still in his golden tomb,
forgotten now the rivers of blood he spilled
sating the parched thirsty desert spoil and grit,
folk hero smiles benign on brides and grooms
dispensing a blessing, that idol's fingers.
Cruelty forgiven and tyranny forgot, absolved,
Bad bloody history seen through tinted lens.

And then we come to Registan that square
Vast Heaven's antechamber, the gate of glory,
Pillars, domes, pilasters, its porticoes ablaze,
all soaring high, all richly iridescent lit,
sumptious as a rainbow turned to stone
shrinking us down to seeming tiny fleas
scurrying within kaleidoscope spellbound
beauty casting its veil on evils of the past.

In Drumnaph Wood

Nine years in war they silent witness stand
verdant youths in spring in autumn dying gold
summer's rustling robes all murmurous green
the dagger tears of winter's drip-dripping ice
encircling ferny raths of old the derry turns
hiding place for Gaelic gallowglass and kern.

Nine years in war they stand and silent watch
sly eyes peek round the solid ivied trunks
heads severed off and bloody bodies fall
trees silent hear the burdened breath of men
heavy their armour-plated panoply of war
the screams, sobs, shouts of Gael and Gall.

When peace it comes earls fleeing Kin/sail
no peace for gentle innocents those oaks
wood cutters, sawyers, axe men axed and cut
holocaust of humble timber to bondage sold
hatchets hacked spliced planks that fall
new turned to gates in other Derry's wall.

If now you walk through Drumlamph Wood
and stand 'neath outstretched arms of oaks
remember victims of that war which we forgot
feel raindrops cold drip drop from leaves
hear echoed sylvan voices crossing years
those sobbing orphaned oaks, their tears.

Footnote: *In 1593 Hugh O'Neill Earl Tyrone led a rebellion against Queen Elizabeth that started the Nine Year's War which ended in defeat in the Battle of Kinsale and the Flight of the Earls. Ulster was the scene of much of the war. The huge oaks forests in Ulster provided cover for rebel Gaelic kerns. Following the slaughter in that war Ulster was pacified and then planted under James I. Huge swathes of the great Ulster forests were felled and the wood used in the plantation and in the building of the English navy. Drumlamph Wood is a tiny remnant of what was once a mighty forest. The oak woods of Ireland are remembered in the word Derry (Doire in Irish).*

FAREWELL TO TURF

memories unlocked not by new ground coffee beans
or bacon sizzling in a pan or by Proust's madeleine
but by circling swirls of turf fresh burned
clinging to the tweedy fabric of the western land
secular incense that flows from chimney thuribles
sliced like chocolate brownies from yielding earth
stacked earthen lumps built up like Irish pyramids
left out to dry beneath the grey and leaden skies
high piled creel carried waiting for sparks and flames
to set free those scented spectres from the past
poignant puncturing stabs of unforgetting grief
homes tumbled ships laden those tears so bitter wept
poor man's brown coal that burns to whitened ash
transubstanced emptiness from seeming solid earth
gone up in smoke leaving more than a hint of a scent
hanging in the air like a long lingering farewell
now burning out those fires slán leat a mhóin a chara

Yvonne Hamilton

A retired primary school teacher living in the seaside town of Portstewart in Northern Ireland, Yvonne Hamilton has been a member of the North Coast Writers for two years. She started to write when forced to retire from a small amateur orchestra when poor night vision made it unsafe for her to travel to rehearsals. That gave her the time – her dogs gave inspiration. In 2022, Yvonne read her own work at Portstewart Library in Northern Ireland as part of the *Aging Gracefully* Initiative. Her work was published in the Anthology *Love, Loss and Cardiac Issues,* Impspired Press, 2022 and *Fetch* a collection of short stories published by Impspired press 2023.

The Wave (1)

The wave that began well out to sea
Swells as it charges towards the shore
Thunders in mists of grey green power
Pushed by the wind that landward blows
Spiralling curls and crashing goes
Breaking on rocks that firmly stand
Tossing the stones up towards the land
Hurling them up sucking them back
They grumble and tumble together click clack

The wave that began well out to sea
Long strings of seaweed orange brown
Tore from the rocks were careless thrown
On to the shore
Piled in a bank to groan and sigh
Awaiting a wave to lift it high
To float for a moment not to dry
But sink to a bed of shell and sand
No nearer sea   no nearer land

The wave that began well out to sea
Grows as it travels towards the land
Thunders wind driven up the strand
No rocks or stones to slow it down
Full force against the hill is thrown
Almost to reach the marram grass
That holds the shifting sand in place
Base of the hill it sweeps away
To lie on the seabed in the bay

Symphony of sea and shore
All well-rehearsed   all played before
Yet never quite the same

After (2)

A cloudless sky. A sea that's calm and still
A gentle breeze drives soft sand towards the hill
Where high above the beach the marram grass
Whistles and bows and bends to let it pass
Full tide meanders silent up the beach
Without the wind and wave it will not reach
Where raging sea sliced half the hill away
To dance on ocean floor out in the bay

The sea out in the bay lies velvet smooth
Only at water's edge is seen to move
To babble, ripple, lap against the rock
That firmly stands unmoved but cannot block
The trickling water gurgling on its way
To join again the ocean in the bay
Before the sun, noon-bright, heats up and dries
All under blazing blue relentless skies

The stones that the wave has tumbled click and clack
Lay then in mounting splendour shining black
The warm soft wind blows in across the bay
Drying their bright black beauty turns them grey
Long strings of seaweed still quite brown and slick
Lie in a tangled pile where sea birds pick
For tiny creatures trapped in the twisted mound
Before it dries, sea bounty to be found

Symphony of sea and shore
All well-rehearsed
All played before
But never quite the same

Remembrance

He stands there alone
In the poppy day sun
Alone in the crowd
The last to remember
All others are gone

He remembers the rain
Its net curtain swirls
In pewter grey sky
That shrouded the earth
Incessantly thrown

He remembers the mud
That squelched under foot
That sucked at the boot
That devoured the blood

He remembers the fear
The foot on the ladder
The shared cigarette
Awaiting the order - over the top
Surrounded by others
Companions and yet
Completely alone.

He remembers the pain
Torn flesh
Shattered bone
That the needle suppressed
But hasn't quite gone
That's waiting to pounce

How he longed to be home.

Alone

I was sitting alone opposite the ice-cream shop, my back to the bay which shimmered in the warm sunshine – just sitting. My attention was drawn to an old couple who, having purchased their ice-cream cones, shuffled across the street to sit down at the other end of my bench. He unzipped his navy anorak. She settled her handbag on her knee before starting to lick round the melting cone to stop it dribbling down the front of her pink cardigan.

She looked round, sighing. *It's good to get the weight off my feet.* She set to work again on the melting ice cream. *This is my favourite seat. Have you noticed it is the only seat not facing the sea - the only seat where we can sit to watch the world go by?*

A long empty pause.

He licked his ice-cream and placed the newspaper, which had been under his arm, across his knee.

Have you ever noticed that old people very often seem to walk with their knees bent? Do you think that's why so many fall?.

He grunted and unfolded his paper.

A long empty pause.

A family ambled by, threading a path through the crowds.

Have you ever wondered why so many people trail their children up and down the street and in and out of shops on a beautiful Sunday?

"What's that?" he muttered, opening up his paper, his ice-cream long gone.

I haven't seen a seagull today. I wonder if they keep watch during the day and meet at night to picnic on the crisps and biscuits and sweets and ice-cream cones we leave behind.

She finished her ice-cream, dropping the end of the cone on the footpath. A contribution to the seagull picnic. ……. presumably.

He shook his paper and turned to a new page.

Have you ever wondered how dogs feel when they are surrounded by a forest of legs moving round them? I wouldn't like to be a dog.

He gave her a sideways glance and remained silent.

"Have you ever noticed that fat people seem to wear very tight clothes nowadays?" I…………

"For goodness' sake, woman! Can't you see I'm trying to read my paper!"

Time to go I thought. Before I reached the crossing I heard, wind-blown in my direction,

Have you ever……..?

Roy

Our first dog was called Scamp. After Scamp my parents were loathe to have another dog. I think they wanted the freedom to come and go as they liked without having to place the dog before any journey could be undertaken. However, with the arrival of Spud in my house they rediscovered the joy a dog could add to their lives as I arrived at their home one day to find them playing with a new pup. There was no debate over the naming of this animal. He had already been named Roy. Roy was a short haired terrier – white with a black head. He was small. In no time at all he became Wee Roy.

Wee Roy was a lively dog, not very clever but good with children and got on with Spud. The two dogs would play happily at their favourite game of tug the floor cloth, one at either end pulling hard and growling. Wee Roy was not as interested in retrieving but did not like to see Spud have the fun all to himself so he would chase the ball to take it away from Spud but had no interest at all in returning it to the bowler.

Wee Roy was cat-like in character, a bit aloof and independent. He was not one to cuddle up if allowed on the sofa though he would lie close to warm up if the room was chilly. He really did not like to be cold. While still quite young found that if he lay on top of the dining room table just under the window the sun warmed him up beautifully. That was his afternoon post while in the evening he lay along the back of the sofa in the lounge to make the most of the evening sunshine. Both locations had the added bonus that he could keep an eye on all the comings and goings outside. In the evening when the fire was lit he lay on the hearth as close to the heat as possible – sometimes so close, in fact, that he had to be pulled away to avoid him going up in smoke!

As was the custom with all dogs that we had over the years Wee Roy was let out at bedtime long enough to 'do his business'. In the cold weather this was a problem for Wee Roy. Being ushered out into a cold dark garden from a warm house made no sense to him and, in the early days, he refused to go so my father had to carry him out, dump him in the garden, run in and shut the door before Wee Roy could nip back in.

As my father had no enthusiasm for these cold nocturnal jaunts either he developed a routine that saved him the trouble. Come bed-time he called Wee Roy and set off to run through the house to the back door making growling noises and shouting 'Where is that cat Roy? Get those birds' so that by the time the back door was reached Wee Roy was barking and frantic to dash out to catch any cat or bird that might be lurking in his garden. It worked every time! It was assumed that, by the time he came in, he had 'done his business'.

My mother had been brought up on a farm and always managed to have a vegetable garden attached to any house in which she lived. She eventually prevailed on my father to provide a green house. He was bit of a DIY person and decided to build a lean-to greenhouse himself at the back of the house off the kitchen. Over one spring and summer my father laid down the foundations, built the low walls before installing the wooden framework that would support the glazing. This work was completed at weekends and in the evenings during the better weather when the days were long but with the arrival of winter all work ceased.

The following spring glass was ordered, my father enlisted friends to help and one day the green house was glazed. My father was proud of his handiwork. My mother was delighted with her greenhouse.

That evening at bedtime when my father had completed his growling and 'get those birds' routine he opened the back door and Wee Roy charged straight out to jump over the green house wall, over the garden wall into the field behind the house. No one had told him about the glass. There was an almighty crash of breaking glass. We ran towards the greenhouse. Was Wee Roy impaled on the broken glass, was he lying cut to ribbons in the greenhouse, was he outside bleeding to death? One section of glass was in bits and there was no sign of Wee Roy in the greenhouse. There was so sign of him in the garden. Was he dead in the field? Just as my father turned to fetch his torch to look for Wee Roy he bounced up on the garden wall and jumped down into the garden wagging his tail. There was not a mark on him. He had been travelling so quickly that he sailed right through the glass unharmed.

A stone's throw from my parents' house a neighbour kept hens in his back garden. There was a henhouse inside a fair sized run that was fenced off with chicken wire. The fence was secure enough to keep the hens in but, as we found out when the owner of the hens came calling, not robust enough to keep Wee Roy out. Wee Roy had managed to get in, cause havoc amongst the chicken community without actually killing any, and get back out again. Apologies were made and assurances given and the chicken man departed. Some discussion followed and it was agreed that if it happened again serious consideration would have to be given to Wee Roy's future. I knew what that meant!

When my parents went on holiday a couple of months later I was left in charge of Wee Roy. Early one afternoon a loud knocking on the door heralded the arrival of a furious chicken man. Wee Roy had killed one of his hens. I knew that something had to be done. If Wee Roy had enjoyed chasing a hen to death once it stood to reason that he would repeat the entertainment. I assured the chicken man that I would pay for the dead hen provided he brought the corpse to me and he agreed, so the chicken was handed over and I paid the price.

Then I set about teaching Wee Roy that chickens were no fun at all either dead or alive. Holding him by the collar and pressing the dead chicken up against his nose I slapped him on his rear end whilst telling him that **good dogs did not chase chickens** and that he must stay away from them in future. He took his punishment like a man and never looked at another chicken as long as he lived.

The Last Dance

She put the phone down, moved the box of crackers, eased herself carefully into her rocking chair and gazed at her husband till her mind drifted back over the years – back to the first time she saw him.

She had shared a flat near the university with three others. All busy with lectures on various courses during the week but ready to party on Saturday nights. She remembered the hectic preparation for the Hops in the Students' Union: the piles of dresses that accumulated on the beds as they were considered and rejected; the rush for the iron before someone else got it; the piles of makeup scattered on all the surfaces in the bedroom; the queue at the bathroom; the swapping of petticoats; the borrowing of shoes. All this accompanied by the drone of hair dryers in the building excitement as the hair was back combed and sprayed firmly in place before the short walk to the union.

It was a mysterious place: – dim-lit, smoke-filled, packed with bodies shouting above the rhythmic thump of the music that vibrated though the floor into the dancing feet; the centre of the floor always filled with open necked shirts and swirling petticoats; the walls hidden by the crowds waiting to be asked or waiting to ask.

That night they pushed their way to their usual meeting place – a place to which they returned between dances, a place where they appeared to belong if no-one asked them to dance. It was important not to look alone, unwanted. She had returned from two dances, both with regulars, friends from her course, who danced with her every week, when she saw him standing between two chatting groups. He was looking at her and she knew, she knew that he would ask her to dance. She knew, she knew that she would accept.

He held her hand as they threaded their way to join the heaving mass of bodies and held her close as they moved to the music. She thought he must surely hear the frantic beating of her heart through her cheek pressed close to his shoulder or the hand he held close to his chest At the end of the section he thanked her before she returned to her group. She remembered thinking please come back before someone else asks. He did, as she knew he would and stayed with her for the last dance. The last dance was the important one. Someone might ask to walk you home.

As the final note faded away he put his arm round her shoulder, "I'd like to walk you home." She hoped that the bolt of pure joy that shot through her was hidden behind the smile that lit up her face as she said, "I'd like that too."

The chat on the way was easy – her course, his sport, her family, his home – till they stopped in the small patch of shadow between two streetlights close to the flat. He turned to face her, took her face between his hands and kissed her. A sweet, gentle questioning kiss. A kiss that asked *are you alright, is this alright,* a kiss that lit up her whole being and took her breath away.

He stepped back, hands on her shoulder, to look at her. "Now, am I going to see you again Elizabeth Brown?" Her heart soared with happiness.

Yes. She had always known he was different right from that first look on that first night – wonderfully, magically, excitingly different for all these years.

The sound of the doorbell brought her back. She struggled up and headed to the door stroking him gently on the cheek as she went. They burst in with their bags, their badges, their uniforms, stamping the snow off their feet and brushing against the Christmas tree so that the decorations jangled. She shut the door against the flashing lights.

"I phoned," she said "He's in the sitting room."

"It's too late," she whispered.

Helen Hand

A rogue Scot living in Dublin, Helen Hand is a retired IT Professional and although computer savvy she prefers to write with a pen. Always having written, she loves words and the surprises which appear when the ink hits the page. Her prose and poems feature in *Pen to Paper*, an anthology by Lucan Creative Writers (2016), in a Chapbook produced by Tallaght Library (2021) and in the anthology *Love, Loss and Cardiac Issues* published by Impspired Press in 2022. Her poem *Window on Beara* was shortlisted for the *The Jonathan Swift Creative Writers Awards,* held in Dublin, *December 2022.*

Peru 1980

They came home   the seven of them

leaving my man behind on the mountain

on a glacier   in a foreign land

he fell so they said

in dreams I didn't believe them

in dreadful dreams   he chose not to come home

tired of me   tired of our children

so he stayed in Peru   lived free loved free

left us   willingly

in daylight   my mind knew the truth of his death

but I took against those others

who left him behind

as if they had helped him to stay there

and knew another truth

The Loch

Old couple sit on
a bench in spring
wrapped and warm
r e m e m b e r I n g
surveying the loch they skated in youth
where each in bladed boot had
swooped and swirled in clockwise circuits

arms linked hearts in sync
young man daring backward skating
leading
his trusting lady in delightful f i g u r e / eights

Molly And Ted

after Pam Ayres

In a few years' time when I'm old and grey
and on the Late Late with that new man – not Gay
I'll happily tell how it came to be
that my book is published and I'm on TV

it began with the stories I'd write in my bed
to a dolly called Molly and a bear called Ted.
I'd write them with crayons of rainbow hue
and Ted marries Molly   the way you do.

In my teens I wrote reams for the boy of the day
declaring my ardour   turned out he was gay.
I ran off to London to work in the smoke
writing code for computer folk.

I wrote letters home to family and friends
homesick and lonely until at the end
they made me redundant   what a gift   praise be
I toddled back North to my own family

In a concrete jungle just north of Glasgow
I fell for a darling and sweet Irish beau
moved to Dublin   we married   had two little babies
    he fell to his death in Peruvian Andes

My writing then was a great resource
not for publication, of course
full of ranting and raving, bewailing my fate
and the language! Oh my god it was great

I effed and I blinded, I c'd and I b'd
I railed at the heavens and I cursed God's deed
but at last it was done and calm was restored
I cast out my pencils I lay down my sword

Well now I'm a granny to the lovely wee Hana
I've taken up writing again in this manner
I don't use crayons or write in my bed
but I do tell of Molly the dolly and Ted

Art to Art   Heart to Heart

I

I see you young man
across the glass café
your coffee long cold
pushed aside to the edge
the very edge of the table

notepad propped
on a stack of books
your pencil darts
ranging up and down
shading and skating surely

you puzzle over your subject
head cocked at the page
swapping 2H for 2B
rubbing a finger
shading   I imagine

I see *you* young man
loving your craft
lost in it
absorbed

II

I see *you* old lady
hunched at your corner table
coffee cup   crumbs
pushed aside to the edge
the very edge of the table.

you lean in
frowning thoughtful
pen poised over paper
then hand and arm
moving   rhythmically

you observe and scribble
throw aside a wasted pen
rush another from your bag
to catch the thought
an elusive word   I imagine

I see you old lady
as I record your form
shading your lines
catching your joy

I see you

Window on Beara

beyond the glass the grassy landscape
edged by hedge and stone dikes
soft dotted with brush and furze
here and there homestead barn and bothy

beyond the glass and greengrass
the gash of blue green sea green flat calm water
waiting for the wind
to whip it into frothy frenzy

beyond the glass greengrass gash of sea
the shore gives way to rising ground
cliffs like bites from abandoned bread
left to rot and dry

beyond the glass greengrass gash of sea
and cliffs of stained teeth rising
the majesty of roaring soaring hilltops
purple proud pushing clouds
resisting their mistiness

beyond the glass greengrass gash of sea
cliffs in rictus hilltops spreading
sprawling breastlike skyward
beyond these known unseen

the jagged skyline of the unknown Reeks

Brendan Magee

From County Fermanagh, a retired civil servant who served in London, Belfast, Liverpool, Manchester, Brendan Magee now lives in Coleraine in Northern Ireland. A member of North Coast and Flowerfield Writers Groups, his work includes the play *McGarrigle's Field*, performed by 'Spring Chickens', a subgroup of Big Telly Drama Group, on March 9th, 2015.

His story *Living Up To The Name* was published in *The Bramley Anthology vol 2,* The Bramley Press, 2020, and a reading of it at Armagh Festival can be found on YouTube, June 2019. His Flash Fiction story, *The Ring,* was published in Flash Fiction Magazine, November 2019. The short stories *Rescue with a flip and a smile, The Real You, Me, Her, Him,* and *Still Serving* featured in the Anthology *Irish Hares and Seahorse,* and *The Last Call* in the Anthology *Love, Loss and Cardiac Issues,* both published by Impspired Press, 2022.

Turf War

Winter used to be my favourite season. The reduced working hours in my ice-cream van provided an early doors pint or two before the open turf and log fire in the Flying Leprechaun. In at four o'clock got one of the two armchairs closest to the heat.

It was about five o'clock. I was on the second pint and a quiet doze. The door burst open, well pushed open. It was a raid, the Material Enforcement Police (MEP) not to be confused with the MET or Member of European Parliament. All two of them, notebook and pen at the ready, strolled to the fire. Wood on the fire was banned and turf associated with criminal activity.

I was charged with obtaining benefit, two warm legs, from the illegal substance and offered a fixed penalty of £50 (£25 for each leg). I said that was unfair, no equality. The leg nearest the fire was always going to get the most heat. I was offered community service as an alternative. Six hours and twenty minutes spying to spot any illegal slurry spreading, overalls, mask and fake tree provided. I paid the fixed penalty.

Tommy the barman was fined £60 and two bottles of house red for distributing illegal material. He had used six foot of timber and three creels of turf. He paid up. Bar proceeds were down that week.

The biggest penalty went to the Giant Quinn, owner of the pub. He was done for supplying illegal material and smuggling from the EU. He had nicked a tractor trailer of turf from a bog bank owned by a priest in Leitrim. Giant denied it was a crime claiming he was using the turf to produce enough ashes for a diocese for Ash Wednesday. He offered samples for forehead marking to the 2 MET but they declined being atheists.

Giant agreed to community service rather than a £200 fine. He had to repatriate the turf. The Customs at the border stopped him with five wheelbarrow loads. They charged him with turf smuggling, ignoring his claim that he was just returning material. An officer tried to set fire to one clod. It wouldn't light, proving that it was Ulster bog turf so the Customs said.

Giant Quinn spread the barrow loads in a line over both sides of the border sprinkling a drop of petrol over the turf. He lit a match and ran like hell. The fire services from both sides arrived in ten minutes but couldn't agree who should lead. They spent the next half hour spray fighting each other. The fire created a no man's land twenty yards either side of the border. The EU is still discussing where the actual border is.

Giant sent us all a postcard from St Kitts. I put mine in the fire. No more winter for me. Spring is my favourite. I now have a stall in Brussels selling Lough Melvin trout with a ten per cent reduction if you guess the nationality.

Footnote:-

Ireland is divided.

There is Northern Ireland and not Northern Ireland. There is dispute about the actual border and location, EU or not EU membership, and especially in relation to this piece, there is dispute about the use of fossil fuels and its related costs.

Fire on, four months to winter.

Deal payment

I rake beneath the cherry tree
search the gooseberry,

strawberry dotted hedge

sweep the pump house floor
recover the funding empties
three lemonades
two brown
one white
two cream sodas
payment for the latest fishing fly

The last hour before dusk
I sit in the single seat
glacier carved stone boat
Sonaghan
Gillaroo
show no appearance upstream

Beating the fall of light
I downstream
stepping Scott's falls
the brown trout hiding
too smart to rise

I pack the rod
for another week
time to search
source another payment.

Blackpool '61

Gracie when we go to chip shop I just want mushy peas.

Why Albert?

I've lost me teeth.

Lost your teeth.

Aye.

How come?

When we got off bus I bought a stick of rock.

I **told** you not to have rock.

But I was only having a lick when me teeth got stuck.

You should only suck. But how'd you lose your teeth?

I took them out to get rock off 'em. I set 'em down in me hanky and a seagull swooped down and flew off with them.

A seagull flew off with your teeth?

Aye.

Well go to the foot of our stairs. Did you not chase it?

Chase it. I was in army not airforce. Anyway it was probably heading to Isle of Man.

Why? Are they short of teeth there?

No it would have been too far to fly onto Ireland.

Are they short of teeth in Ireland?

Aye. They've been training seagulls and pigeons to steal teeth.

Who told you that?

I read it in Daily Sketch.

Well I never.

Could I borrow your teeth in the chippy?

No. You never wash your hands you dirty bugger. But I know what. Let's go to the pawn shop and buy a set.

Will they have some?

Oh aye. Me dad used to pawn his teeth every week for five shillings. How much have you got.

Fifteen shillings and ten pence.

Oh that'll be plenty.

See Sam with that floozy. He promised her a bag of chips if she'd sit on his knee.

And piece of rock salmon.

I hope she pours the salt and vinegar on him, not the chips.

Right, which way to pawn shop? We'll have a pot of whelks on the way.

I'll have a ride on the donkey later.

God help it.

Divine

O' Brady had a skill that you would never detect from his appearance. He rode the countryside on a bike that he had inherited from his father and irrespective of the weather in a overcoat and flat cap that could have come from his grandfather. On the days he wanted, he travelled the roads at a speed as if he was the doctor out on some emergency call. But those days were few. Winter he'd spend half the day in bed and the evening out to ceile at neighbours for a mug of tea and half a currant loaf. Summer was spent staring at the bog bank as if the turf would cut itself. Some said he was composing poetry but it must have been in his head as no one ever discovered any written verse. It was a miracle that he had saved a cart load by the end of September.

He came from a long line of farmers but would be the last. He had no interest in land or cattle, nor women for that matter. But he was a wanted man. He had to be booked well in advance and even then there was no guarantee that he would show up a week either side of the agreed date.

Arriving at breakneck speed as if a matter of life or death and jump off the bike leaving it to career on its own or until it came to a halt in the nearest ditch or hedge. A man of few words. 'Where?' O'Brady would head as directed. When he arrived in the nominated field, reach into the inside pocket of the coat and take out the forked twig.

With a hand on each fork, he'd hold the twig as if a championship cup and crisscross the field. Acolytes came to watch but at a respectful distance just in case they interrupted the power.

There was no guarantee of success and sometimes appointments would have to be made for another field. The majority of visits ended in detection. At the point of discovery he would fight the twitching twig as if wrestling with a demon. Then in triumph O'Brady would stab the stick into the ground with the force of driving a stake into Dracula's heart. 'Here, water' was all he would say as he headed into the house for payment and the tea.

Many admired his power but I don't recall anyone matching it. I tried it once myself and spent two hours walking up and down the big meadow without any success. I threw the forked twig into the river but even then it didn't twitch.

Forgotten

Buried
by the
undertaker and
church caretaker
without whisper or
whimper

No hymns
no gentle organ
no flowers
just a
pauper's coffin

An aged man
alone
forgotten and
unthanked
for service unspoken
and memories
suppressed
Society said
Amen.

Brenda McAteer

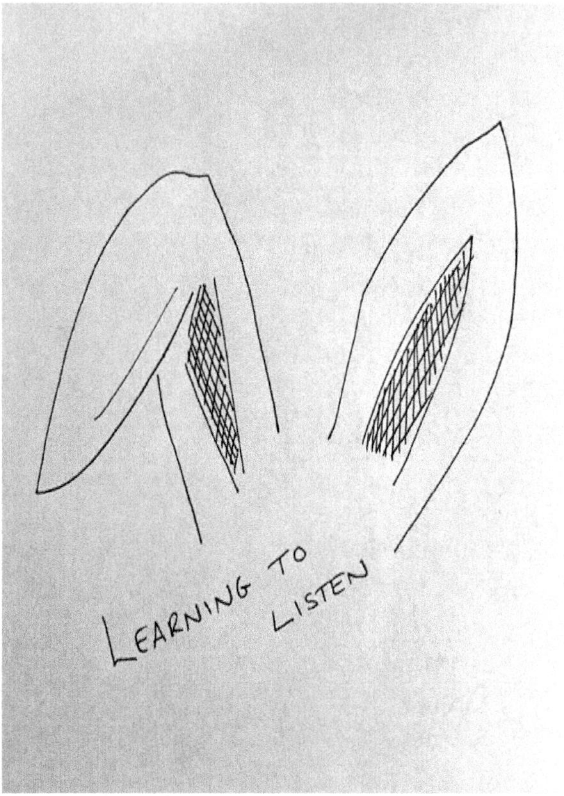

Living in Portrush, a seaside town in Northern Ireland, Brenda McAteer joined North Coast Writers in January 2020 after she retired. Stories had wandered round her head as she worked full time and raised three sons. With NCW support they are now appearing on paper. A Flash Fiction piece *No Walk No Escape* was performed at the Orchard Flash Festival, 2021 and can be found on YouTube www.byddilee.com/flash-fiction-armagh. In 2022, a memoir piece *Watch Cup* was published by Northworld NI, as well as two pieces in *100 Voices - NI 100 Years,* BCRC. Also in 2022, her work was published in the North Coast Writers Anthology *Irish Hares and Seahorses* and in the Anthology, *Love, Loss and Cardiac Issues,* both published by Impspired Press. A Flash Fiction piece Reflections was performed at A Night at the Museum 2023 and can be found on www.byddilee.com/flash-fiction-saturday-night-in-the-museum-2023

Irish Rain

Mizzle is like
floating through mist
soft and light
not really wet

Drizzle dampens
gentle vapour spray
fine drops linger
feels soggy

Showers falling
steady even droplets
rainwear needed
getting wetter

***Bucketing* down**
blinded by giant drops
gushing in sheets
totally drenched

SQUALLS FLING TORRENTS
SUDDEN GUSTS OF WIND
SIDEWAYS LASHES
SOAKED AND SMARTING

***An attempt to explain Irish rain to*
*my Spanish Daughter-in-Law***

~~~
~~~

Thirteen Seconds

One second

My baby girl roaring at me, shouting about her rights to go out half naked. Lucy, my diamond in the sky, aged fifteen. Doesn't want a lift home, she'd die of embarrassment if I turned up. I can't cope. Head and chest tight. Those onions at dinner too much. I take some Gaviscon, go and lie down.

Two seconds

Marianne's back from taking her mother to the consultant. Her face tells it all. I can see it's not good news. I let her cry in my arms. It's dementia. We need to start planning for Sadie's care. I go upstairs and try to calm down. Heart racing, I feel so fatigued. Splash water on my face, sit down, breathe slowly. Downstairs to offer my support.

Three seconds

The asshole of a new manager called me in today. I need to up my callouts to at least 25 a week! I'm the engineer requested by most clients because I take time over the job, listen to their woes and tidy up. What would he know? He's never been out on an actual job. In the car on the way home I start to shake, feel nauseas, sweat. My hands are glued to the wheel. I pull in, lean back, breathe slowly. Normality returns.

Four seconds

Sunday family lunch out. Lucy and Sadie on the same wavelength, a joy to watch them playing the silly games they did when Lucy was little. After lunch we go for a walk in the rose garden. Sadie clinging to Lucy. 'Slow down a bit', I call. Too late, they both take a tumble. Lucy in hysterics. I rush to help but get the most painful cramp and indigestion ever and lie curled up beside Sadie. In the end, just scratches and scabs, no broken bones. We all have a laugh about it on the way home.

Five seconds

Marianne complains about the amount of Gaviscon I'm taking. She's also annoyed about how tetchy I've become. I shout, 'It's stress - pressure of work, negotiating a teenager, trying to get help for your Mum to keep her at home'.

'Me too', she wails. I storm off. Halfway up the stairs I double in two and half sit, half lie on the stairs. 'Right' she announces, 'You're going to the Doctor'.

Six Seconds

'Don't see you often Mark. What's the problem?' I mutter about work, teenagers, poorly mother-in-law. He checks blood pressure, heart rate, a bit high but not bad. 'There's no need to do a BMI, you're so slim'.

'I swim 40 lengths two or three times a week'.

'It's not your heart then, Mark, stress probably. I could give you beta blockers but come back in six weeks and we'll repeat the tests, just to be sure'.

Seven Seconds

The long-planned summer holiday in Alicante. Marianne's brother has moved in with Sadie for the week. Sun, sea, siestas. A trip in a glass bottomed boat to glimpse the sea life. So colourful, just gorgeous. Without warning I'm gripped by panic. Sweat pouring down my face and body. I clench Marianne's wrists in an attempt not to keel over. Back to the hotel, a cool shower and siesta sorts me out.

Eight Seconds

We're visiting potential care homes for Sadie. Two pleasant and caring but the third we wouldn't have left a stuffed cat in. The so-called adult care manager makes my work boss look considerate! All about money. There's the monthly fee, but any extras like hair dressing and outings will be charged separately. I shout, 'Can she pee for free', as I storm to the car in a rage and collapse at the wheel. I gasp for breath and pour sweat. Marianne glares at me.

Nine Seconds

'Me again Doc, now having panic attacks.' He listens, checks me out, all readings a bit higher but then I'm so stressed. He refers me on to Cardiology. Just in case.

Ten Seconds

I have such a row at work with my manager. He's suggesting that at fifty-seven I should look at my options. Early retirement or an office job. I fume and go into a bit of a frenzy. Storm to the car, speed off, scrape the side panel exiting the carpark. Shout at Marianne and stamp off to bed – at 7pm.

Eleven seconds

Doc phones after I ask for a sick line. So uptight after the row with the manager I take a week off. First time in forty years at the firm. Doc says he's been speaking to Cardiology and if I have another panic attack I've to go straight in as that's the best time to take readings.

Twelve seconds

We've chosen a care home. We're going to tell Sadie. I'm driving but feeling so anxious for Marianne. How are we going to convince Sadie this is good news? We stop at the last set of lights before Sadie's house and I freeze. Cars behind blaring their horns but I can't move. Heart and head pounding, sweat pouring. Marianne gets the driver behind to help drag me into the back seat. She speeds to the Cardiology Department.

Thirteen Seconds

I vaguely agree to an exercise ECT. Hooked up to the machine the nurse instructs me to start walking. "Let's see how many minutes you can march", she smiles.

Thirteen seconds - that's all I achieve before the nurse stops the machine, throws me in a wheelchair and takes me to the cardiac ward. Later Marianne, white as my bedsheet says, "Those weren't panic attacks Mark. More like mini heart attacks. Warnings your heart was failing – you could have died".

All my future seconds

Angina. I have angina. It all makes sense now. Can't have a stent fitted but with lifelong medication I can batter on as normal.

Not only feeling fit but I've stopped bawling at my shadow - and all my loved ones.

My Union have told work I need less stress, so I'm back to my original workload. Asshole scared to upset me, result!

My GP apologises every time we meet. He says I've reminded him slim, non-smokers who exercise can still have heart issues. Genetics and all that.

Best of all, Lucy now calls me Lucky Thirteen. She works hard to avoid setting up major incidents at home. She says she just wants to keep my heart ticking.

So do I.

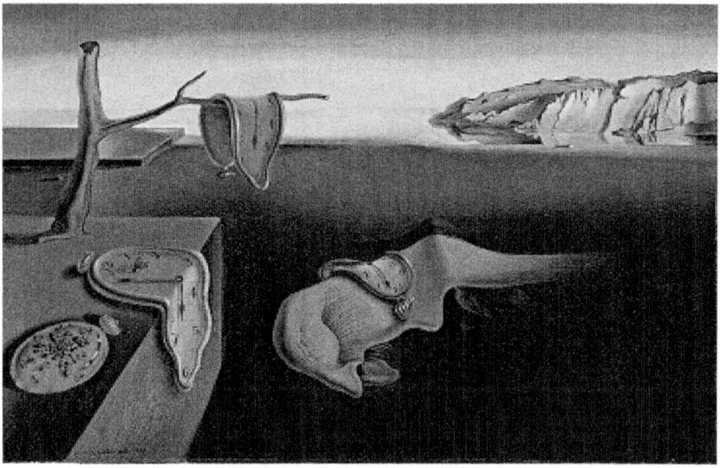

The Persistence of Memory by Salvador Dali

Ticking Away

~after 'The Persistence of Memory' by Salvador Dali ~

Lucy asks to be taken to a room with no time. The nurses look at her with sympathy,

'What do you mean Lucy?'

'I want a room with no clocks, no watches, no phone, no radio, no TV. No way of counting the seconds, the minutes, the hours. There are no church bells near here, are there?

'No Lucy, but why do you want this?'

'I want to exist in my own time, in my own head. I want rid of the relentless marching of time led by others steering me. I agreed to come here of my own volition to have space and calm. To stop hurting myself. To find time to heal without clocks and their seconds, minutes, hours'.

The nurses open the door to her room. Small, with a single bed, desk, adjoining toilet and shower. Everything fixed so she could be kept safe.

She looks around, then asks,

'Could the clock and the TV be removed, please?'

'They're screwed to the wall, but I could get the clock battery removed and cover both with brown paper. Would that help?'

She nods.

Left alone she sighs, lies on the little hard bed, closes her eyes. She remembers a poster of a painting by Dali she had stared at, mesmerised for an age. *The Persistence of Memory*. She brings that image forward.

Clocks draped over objects, clocks melting.

'That's what I want. To put the past times that hurt, that diminished me, on hold. Trap them in their own time. Then melt them away, disintegrate them.'

Over the next few weeks, she works with a counsellor to bring those images of hurt forward. To draw them, craft them, visualise them.

Father – fierce and frosty, hating all around him. Placed in a plain, dark clock face draped over his pipe rack – fragmenting.

Mother – cowered in a corner, whimpering. Placed in a transparent clock face, hung on a hook behind a door – withering.

School bullies – bound under steel hands on a roast red clock face – smouldering.

She watches them dissolve, she disentangles herself from *their* time. These clock faces are now imprisoned in *their* time, not hers.

She begins to see herself in her time, in control ….

They no longer persist

Their time has gone

Lucy looks forward

Trusting *Lies*

--Farningham People's Park 4pm--

I can't do this any longer. I can't keep pretending. It's just I don't know how to say it. Jeni thinks I'm her strength, her protector, her provider. I'm none of these now.

'My Darren doesn't go home via the pub or bookies, straight back to me. I'm so lucky', she tells her Mum. Jeni and her equally lovely Mum, inseparable.

Too cold to sit here any longer, I'll go to the pub.

--22, Rose Gardens, Setham 6.15pm--

Jeni dashes about. The aroma of the beef casserole fills the kitchen, table set and Bo the dog banished to the utility room. After they married Jeni decided to work mornings only in the Care Home office. This gives her time to have the house spick and span and dinner ready for Darren. The girls in the office rib her about this. She doesn't care, it gives her real pleasure. She glances at the wall clock, Darren's due soon.

It's 6.50, Jeni paces about, chews her fingers, glances out the window. No sign of Darren. She joked with him recently if he wasn't in by 6.30, she'd panic. The builder's suppliers, where Darren works, is close to Farningham station. Since he got promotion, he finishes on the dot at 5.30. It's only a half hour train ride back to Setham and a short walk to their house. She fidgets, turns off the cooker and decides to take Bo and walk towards the station. Bo looks confused. Jeni pats her and says, 'We're going to meet Darren from the train. An early evening walk, rather than after dinner as usual, come on Bo'. Happy with her lead on, they head off.

On the way to the station Jeni spots Dan who works with Darren. 'Just walking to meet Darren,' she says as they pass. 'He must have missed the 5.40'. Dan looks a bit bewildered, just nods and rushes on.

--The Lion and Bear Farningham 5.50pm--

Oh God, I've missed the 5.40 train. I'm going to be late back. I've been sitting here in a stupor. I'm so weary doing nothing. Over an hour in here and only one cup of coffee, no wonder the barmaid's scowling at me. The days are feeling longer, there's no purpose, I'm just avoiding the inevitable. Bile rising, Darren rushes to the men's and throws water on his face.

'Look at us,' Jeni trills to me, 'Our own little house, enough to live on and just so cosy. Everything I ever dreamed of Darren. Mum struggled on her own to raise Jamie and me. She worked all hours, three different part time jobs at one time. Jamie and I had to mind each other, sometimes just jam butties for tea. This isn't a castle, but it's ours'.

How can I destroy her dreams? She's even talking of us trying for a baby now we're married three years - so secure now with my promotion. God, or some other power help me!

--Setham Station 7.05pm--

Jeni greets Tim, the guard, and asks when the next train from Farningham is due.

'About half an hour Jeni, but your Darren got off at 6.55. Head down and marching for the crossing. Doesn't really chat to me anymore.'

Jeni tries not to look shocked, thanks him, burbling that he must have walked through town, not the back lanes. Feeling queasy and shaky she drags Bo to the street. She looks up and down – home or town?

'Let's walk to town Bo maybe he's gone to buy a magazine or flowers.' Not that he's surprised me with flowers for ages, she sighs.

--Bench on Church Street, Setham 7.05pm--

I'll buy some flowers, a waste of money, but I'll need something to give her even if she flings them back at me. How could I have thought keeping this farce up would help. I'm such a coward. I get up at 7 each morning, shave, shower put on that excuse for a suit. Grab my lunch, kiss Jeni and head off to the station. Monthly ticket to Farningham - such a waste of money but I can't risk being seen wandering round weekdays in Setham. Three months, ninety-two days since they called me in and made me redundant. Sixty-six working days.

The Manager called me up to his office. He spoke to the desk, not me, and announced in a cold, hard voice, 'Darren, you're surplus to requirements now we've installed the new IT system. It's the way of the world I'm afraid. You'll get twelve weeks pay for redundancy and another twelve if you agree to leave at the end of the week'.

Twelve years and I'm replaced by a computer. I couldn't go home and tell her, wreck her world. In a flash of insane lightening I announced that I'd got promotion and would be home every day by 6.30.

'No need for overtime Jeni, or late nights anymore getting orders sorted'. Oh, the hugs, kisses and congratulations. Then straight on to tell her Mum the good news. Day by day the lies just expand. What was I thinking!

--Walking to Setham Town Centre 7.15pm--

Grasping Bo's lead Jeni tries not to blubber. She tells herself to stop being silly but keeps thinking of April's face when she had excitedly told her about Darren's promotion. April opened and closed her mouth like a fish and then croaked, 'Ah, yeah, great.' Then bolted on. Well she should've known, Jeni thought, she used to work in the manager's office and still hears all the chat.

Feeling uneasy Jeni whispered to her Mum, 'Darren's been a bit strange lately, Mum'.

'For goodness sake Jeni, your Darren is the most reliable man on the planet,' her Mum reassured her.

Even so Jeni was taken aback two weeks ago when he announced, he was going to sell the car. 'Well you don't drive love and the train does me.' She adored that old Mini, their Sunday runs out with her Mum in tow. Her Mum cautioned, 'Well, it's his decision Jeni, he's the driver.'

--Bench on Setham Church Street 7.15pm--

I know I'm a fool but three mornings a week I head to Farningham Library to read the papers, look online for jobs, even doze on the comfy chairs. Those two pensioners prod me for info every day they're in. Getting harder to make up lies that match the last lot I told them. The other two mornings I walk round the rundown shopping mall and sit on the seats for the elderly - until the real elderly turn up. Lunch time off to the park. Just as well there's a couple of covered shelters. Opening my sandwiches and flask all I can see is Jeni's trusting face. Then I just walk – that's why I've lost weight Jeni – it's not the responsibility of the new post. October next week, I can't keep this farce going, I'll freeze soon. Plus, I need to put a plan in place for my dwindling pay-off. Three months of putting the 'housekeeping' in the joint account as usual is draining it. I've got to tell Jeni the truth, but when and how? Right go and buy flowers.

--Tesco Express, Setham 7.20pm--

Jeni drags Bo towards the High Street, then stops, shudders and gasps. She's nearly sure that is Darren going into Tesco Express. Flustered, she bursts through Tesco's automatic doors. He's choosing flowers. They're for me - aren't they? She shakes. Bo barks and leaps towards Darren. He jumps and drops the bunch he'd finally chosen.

Oh, *my God it's Jeni. She's staring at me. She's shivering. Her pale face says it all, she's frightened.*

Cornered, I have no escape.

This is it –

the when –

now –

how?

Marked

Camille, crying, is flung on a trolley and rushed to theatre for an emergency section. I run behind feeling useless. What can a husband do at a time like this? Camille is asleep in seconds. I stand behind the curtain clasping and unclasping my hands, nerves jangling. I try to block out the sickening suction sounds and the commands from doctors to midwife,

'Scalpel.' 'Hold the head'. 'Where's that foot'. Then silence.

~ ~ ~

They thrust the baby into my arms. It's a girl. I wanted a boy. She starts to howl, such a surly screwed up crimson face. I hold her - not too close and stare.

~ ~ ~

There's a strange mark on her hand, what is it? Red and curled. I touch it. It's rough, feels like - like scales. I draw in my breath and look closer. Pressing the scaly smudge, I nearly drop her. Its snake shaped with a perfect triangular head.

I'm hyperventilating. It knows. My heart thumps. How can it? I believe in reincarnation and I'm sure I was a snake in my last life. A magnificent thirty-foot-long, sadistic, powerful python. I terrorised any person -

young, old, strong or weak - that wandered into my domain. I slowly squeezed the life out of them. Such sovereignty in my kingdom.

Life as a human is a crushing disappointment. No power, little control. Camille, a human who has made this incarceration bearable. She can't waken to see this, it's not a human baby, but my burden reborn through this creature.

I press into the mark on its hand, definitely scales. I squeeze harder and its eyes snap open. I gasp, nearly throw it to the floor. I just recover my composure as the midwife smiles over. Those aren't human eyes, my brains squeals. They're green with hazel flecks, but even more alarming, the pupils are vertical slits. Perfect snake eyes.

It's holding me in a defiant glare. I feel the mark on its hand begin to throb. Is it someone from my previous existence, someone I asphyxiated, back for revenge? I need to act. I need to squash life out of this thing now. If I don't it'll destroy me.

'Mr. Janus, your lovely baby girl. Just hand her to me. We need to weigh and measure her……… Mr. Janus don't hold her so tight, ***stop squeezing her***. Mr. Janus hand over your child to me - NOW!'

Orla McFaul

Living with her family in Bellaghy, a Northern Irish village home to the Seamus Heaney Homeplace, after taking courses there Orla McFaul joined North Coast Writers in 2021. She read two of her poems '*Twilight*' and '*Changing Focus*' at the Seamus Heaney Homeplace in 2021. Her poems were published in *Autumn Fragments,* a pamphlet ed. Jessica Traynor, 2021. In 2022 her work was published in *Irish Hares and Seahorse,* a North Coast Writers Anthology, and in the Anthology *Love, Loss and Cardiac Issues,* both published by Impspired Press.

Baking Day

with the smell of fresh baked bread
I am transported
yesterday   or a dozen years

you are at the kitchen window
baking sodas on the griddle

nimble hands moulding the dough
flipping and turning with a deft touch
like a thousand times before

sleeves rolled up to the elbow
your signature look
radio on   you sing
hum along to a mellow country tune

flour dust dancing in the air
a pot of tea   a listening ear

all the time in the world

Conundrum

I wasn't looking for you
I had forgotten you existed
almost

you came back
intense   intent

you seemed to be the answer
to heal my wounds
balm for the boredom

but you were a question   a conundrum
I've been trying to solve ever since

at odds with everything I believe
or thought I believed

to stay or go
the battle rages

inside my mind
and I suspect   inside yours

To Dominic and Ceara 19th April 2022

Our Wish For You

~

Today is a new chapter   its Day One
a bittersweet gathering
we are gaining a daughter   not losing a son

as a child
we nurtured   guided you
the best way we knew

with help along the way
aunts, uncles, grandparents too
all here   proud   or looking down on you

our new daughter and beloved son
fly off   conquer the world
our job is done

we wish you joy   happiness,
peace and
above all love

wherever you wander
wherever you land
always united hand in hand

make your home in each other
with all of us in your heart
that way we'll never be apart

listen to the wise words of others today
walk your own path
forge your own way

Dominic and Ceara
a new Mr and Mrs McFaul
I know you have built **your** *solid wall* x

Footnote – *This poem was read as a reflection at a wedding mass, directly after a reading of Seamus Heaney's poem Scaffolding. The 'solid wall' is in reference to Heaney's poem.*

A Sunday in summer 1986.

~ in both Prose and Poetry ~

I was nine years old. Sundays were very predictable back then. My mother woke first, to prepare for the day and attend eight o'clock Mass. We older kids went with my father to half nine Mass. There were a lot of masses back then! Sunday lunch was early, around one o'clock. A traditional roast dinner, with fresh, home-grown vegetables. Followed by a homemade dessert of apple or rhubarb crumble, or on occasion, something modern and fashionable, such as pavlova or cheesecake. My mother always took a nap afterwards. Seemed to be the only day it was acceptable for her to rest. Then late afternoon, we would visit my grandparents, in Swatragh 10 miles away.

I don't remember exactly how it came about, but, this day, we had decided to walk the journey to my grandparent's house. The back roads, ten miles!

So, my father, two brothers, (eleven and seven) and I, set off on the journey. Three miles in, on a long winding road, my mother pulled up in the car, with my two younger sisters. My brothers jumped into the car. They'd had enough. My father was adamant, he was walking the whole way. I was torn, I wanted to go in the car too. But I didn't want to leave my father on his own. I decided to stay with him. I remember my mother saying *Are you sure now? It's a very long way still.*

I stayed. I'll never forget the sight of that big blue ford meandering its way onwards, on that endless stretch of road …until it became only a dot … and then disappeared.

I don't recall much of the rest of that walk, or what we talked about along the way. My father says I didn't complain. I do remember the feeling of great relief at having my grandparents' big farmhouse in sight… at last. Such a hero's welcome we received, from the many relatives there visiting, cousins, aunts, uncles, my sick dying granny, my grandfather… and my mum.

Fast forward thirty-five years, another Sunday, March 2021. I undertook this pilgrimage again. More of us this time. In memory of my mother, our first Mother's Day since she passed. Her sisters, brothers, children, grandchildren, nieces, nephews and friends all walked or ran the ten miles together. There were also two nine-year-olds, who didn't complain, enjoyed the hero's welcome at the end, just as I had. All those years ago.

A Sunday   Summer 1986

I was nine years old
Sundays were predictable back then
morning mass   roast lunch
visits to my mother's homeplace

this day stands out   the decision   the adventure
my father   my two brothers and I   would walk
the back road   to my grandparents' house
I had no concept of ten miles   didn't sound like much

a few miles in
my mother pulled up in the car with my younger sisters
the boys gladly gave up
I was torn   but determined

the big blue ford   became a tiny dot
then disappeared   on the endless stretch of road
I don't recall much of the rest
my father says I didn't complain

I remember relief at first glimpse   of the farmhouse
the hero's welcome we received
from a sick and wilting granny
cousins   grandad   and my mum

fast forward 35 years   another Sunday
March 2021   Mother's Day
I walked that road for the second time
a pilgrimage   in mother's memory

fifty or so   family and friends
including two nine-year-olds   who didn't complain
enjoyed a hero's welcome at the end
as I had   all those years ago

Jimmy Milliken

Currently living on the north coast of Ireland, Jimmy Milliken grew up in the north of Ireland but spent much of his adult life in the Shetland Islands. He has twice been shortlisted for the Seamus Heaney Poetry Award; in 2018 for his poem "Mercy Killing" and in 2020 for "Lichen". His poem "Colloquy" was shortlisted for the 2020 Bangor Literary Journal 40 Words Competition and appears on YouTube. His poem "The Butt" was longlisted for the 2019 Bangor Literary Journal Poetry Competition. He has performed his poetry at various showcase events in Ireland, including The Seamus Heaney Homeplace in Bellaghy and in Portstewart, Ballymoney, Ballycastle and Limavady, and also most notably on a mountain top in Connemara. His first collection of poetry *Cracking the Air* was published by Impspired Press in August 2022. His poems have been published in every annual CAP Anthology published in Northern Ireland from 2016 until 2022.

on picking up an old book of Modern Irish Poetry

the slightest hint of entropy has crept
between the pages
they're brown around the edges
emitting   faint   an odor of must and dust
the cover illustration   a tumbled round tower
in a graveyard   is faded   gradually
evaporating   into the ether

how long has it been crammed in here between
Rhyme and Reason and *The Collected Poems of James Stephens*

it doesn't seem that long ago I brought it home
and half the team were still alive then
Hewitt   Heaney   and feck it   even Beckett
oh the rage   turn the page   turn the page
even one boy born in 1882 was
still clinging on
while others died young   executed   for their part
in the Easter Rising   or fighting
the fascists in Spain

it opens *Pardon, old fathers, if you still remain*
and ends *they never attack after dark*

and there's many a life in between

put it back   put it back
in the bookcase again

mescal shots

... we weren't lying on the floor staring at patterns on the wall and muttering - *oh wow* - or jumping out of windows screaming - *I can fly!* - or hanging around school gates giving pound deals to children. We were merely sitting round the kitchen table chewing the cud in a most affable manner. Okay, we were also doing mescal shots and Cammie was putting one together. You could say we were out on the margins of polite society. Yeah, and maybe even a bit beyond.

We were certainly beyond the mainland on a small island off a bigger island hundreds of miles from the city without mains electricity, nine-to-five jobs, but we were paying our own way more or less and growing our own food, and at least we weren't bankers or arms dealers or money launderers or politicians.

And I suppose that night we were a little bit out of our heads.

Then Rachel shows with her kids and this friend of hers.

Gibbie brought us in – she says – *Iain's doing the Round Foula. We're going over to Hamnavoe to meet him.*

Rachel made supper for herself and the kids and they sat on the couch and watched telly. None of us knew her friend. She just sat in the corner all meek and mild and didn't speak to anyone. I wondered if she might be a 'born again'.

After a while I says to her - *would you like to join us?*

I've never done mescal - she says.

Just take a pinch of salt on the wrist then knock it back and bite the lime - says Janie.

She catches on no bother.

Oh- she says - *the lime it's so... you know...*

After a couple more shots Cammie skins up again.

Toke? - he says - *finest Lebanese.* And she takes the J.

Like, I don't really smoke - she says and laughs.

Couple more shots and she's telling me about some childhood trauma. It's really heavy stuff. She starts crying, talks a bit more and then she's laughing and taking a toke and - *fuck me, I feel better* - she says -*where's Rachel and the kids?*

They've gone to Hamnavoe to meet the boats - says Belle - *half hour ago.*

It's OK we're all going after this - says Gunnhilda.

Gunnhilda puts her arms round her - *you're such a gentle creature. You're beautiful.* And they sit and hug one another. Gunnhilda, like this blonde Icelandic giantess and her all elfin, dark and delicate.

Yeah - says Rachel's friend - *I feel so good and you*

know I was worried about coming.

Arthur cracks open some beers - *we'll take these and go.*

We walked across the Isle and came up over the hill to Hamnavoe. The sun had just gone down and most of the yachts had already arrived. Just one or two beyond the mouth of the voe, where the Hill o' Fielie and Mauns Hill towered over the passage. Out on the horizon the peaks of Foula misty blue against the peachy sky.

Arthur flung his arms in the air. *Behold! The edge of the world, man. The Ultima Thule.*

As we started down the hill she touched my arm - *you know I never told anyone that before.*

Heavy stuff.

Yeah, but like, I feel I'm not carrying it anymore. It's like I... I dunno... see it differently.

Down below most of the folk had come off the boats. Campfires dotted the shoreline. Thin and wispy lines of smoke drifted into the air and disappeared. Guitars were starting up, fiddles and whistles. Someone had an accordion.

It would be a long night.

Cammie turns to me - *this must be what it's all about...*

the ice

...perhaps it is as if a stranger visits your farm - coming over the hill through the shade of the back lane - the fairy fort - the hawthorns – not the way anyone ever comes...

...it is evening - no later – twilight - not quite night but neither is it the day - an in-between time when you might imagine a crack between the worlds –a breach – deep – dark - through which for a briefness of time there is an opening - when something from outside might creep in...

...this stranger - he has slipped a cloak of familiarity about himself - he looks like anyone - almost like people you know - but if you were to study him closely you could see things are not quite right – clothes dishevelled – badly chosen – poorly matched - don't quite fit - something awkward in the way his limbs move - arms hang loose - legs when he walks are stiff - his movements judder and sway – as if he doesn't quite know how...

...he speaks your language - but the way he uses the words is unusual - not wrong - archaic - stilted - his accent is unfamiliar - not foreign - not local...

...he flatters you - like he is trying to win your trust – he smiles but his eyes are cold – there seems to be something deep inside the pupils that flickers fleetingly - bitter - palest blue…

…and slowly a feeling creeps over you that his whole being is a charade - that all the time the cloak might slip off - that beneath is something unfamiliar - something sinister - not of this world - and you don't really know if he is your friend at all - or what he really wants from you - or what he wants to do with you – as if he lusts after your place in the world - and you will be banished to a twilight realm where you will never feel the warmth of the world again...

...you wake in the morning – for a moment a sense of dread hangs over you – already the vision fading until there is no memory – a dream forgotten...

...and in the light of morning there is a glamour on the world – the window pane frosted – a supernova – a northern forest – a tangle of ferns – all delicate and made of ice – tiny particles of ice – an abiogenesis of ice – stare deep inside each particle – a fractality – a multidimensionality – worlds within worlds...

...and beyond the window this world – brilliant - sparkling - cloaked in white - every branch of every tree drawn in delicate lines of white - hills shrouded - distant mountains so close and yet forever beyond reach - a frozen silent world - shrouded in stillness - sky so pale -

barely a memory of blue - unreal – a dream world...

...Mama Mama - you call - *what has happened to the world...*

...Mama in the kitchen - scents of spice and dried fruit – baking bread - sunlight streams through windows - shines on the china - reflects on copper pans - ignites her golden hair – a flaming angel – the blonde banshee Papa would call her – Papa gone...

...winter is come – says Mama and she smiles - but ever that sadness in her eyes - as if she still remembers something from a long ago time - or maybe from dreams...

...Toby calls rapping the door and demands you join him - *the others are coming too we will meet on the hill above the lake...*

...Toby wrapped in coat and scarf and hat - only his face shows - cheeks pinched with cold - nose and lips almost blue - you barely recognise him - even his voice has all the warmth sucked out of it...

...Mama stands in the doorway waving as you go - with each step the warmth of the house dissipates - and you feel as if Mama is fading – by the time you reach the gate the house and garden seem swallowed in an enormity of ice and snow...

...*stay off the ice* - she calls - *don't go out on the lake...*

...but her voice seems distant - as if it were coming from far away - long ago...

...perhaps you will never forget this moment - Mama framed in the doorway - one hand raised - reaching out to you - but all detail gone from the memory - like an old photograph exposed to years of light - everything faded – almost white - only a hint of grey around the door frame and the interior of the house - and a vague shadow in the doorway - Mama waving – and perhaps even that memory will recede until it becomes no more than the memory of a memory – and finally all there will be is that once a woman watched a boy run down a path in the snow...

...coldness grips you - squeezes tight - directs your thoughts and your thoughts lead you to the hill above the lake...

...as you pass through the orchard you notice something russet on the whiteness – it seems almost to glow - a dead bird – you pick it up - a thrush – big - fat – perfect - the feathers still soft and warm - but beneath stiff - unyielding - you stare entranced at the dark eye – the beak slightly open – the moment of death captured and held...

...from nowhere a breeze rustles through the branches above you - soft and low – a whisper - *it doesn't have to be this way - alone in the snow* - a voice of longing – gentle - compelling...

...you turn to Toby – and you know he has heard nothing – he is looking at the thrush – there is envy upon him - *give it here* - you tighten your grasp – run ahead...

...the others are already on the hill - throwing snowballs - toppling a snowman - kicking lumps of snow out of his enormous head – his grin bursts in a flurry - dancing round him – chanting – stamping – screeching - throwing armfuls of snow in the air – high and wild...

...*give me the bird* - says Toby - *let me show them...*

...you hold it tight - shove it in your pocket...

...*pansy* - he says – *pansy* - he runs to the others - *the pansy's got a bird - he won't hand it over...*

...they surround you - bundle you to the ground - still you refuse to hand over the thrush – Ollie sits on your chest – Faye throws snow in your face...

...*stuff the pansy full of snow* – snow in your mouth - your eyes – down your neck - you struggle - they wrestle - Daniel snatches the bird from your pocket...

...they dance around you throwing the bird from one to another...

...*give it back* - you cry – even to yourself your voice sounds weak - piteous – you are defeated...

...they tear feathers from the bird – anoint you with them – Faye forces a handful of down into your mouth – stifling – choking – taste of earth – decay - you lie there sobbing – they tear off the wings – the legs – the head – drop them on your face...

...*pansy - pansy – pansy* – then bored they turn in search of a new game...

...you struggle to your feet and run – their taunts fade into the distance – you stumble fall – rise and run until you are panting - soaked in a chill sweat in the freezing air – and flop once more into the snow...

... and when you look up you see you are at the side of the lake - it looms before you a huge silent presence – you are shivering - it is colder here – bitterly cold - as if this is the source of all the coldness in the world...

...and you can almost hear a whispering in your ear - *you have been betrayed by Toby – you are alone – friendless - the others were never really your friends - now there is no one – you are alone* – and you do not know if these thoughts are your own – or are they whisperings crackling into your mind from outside...

...you stare out across the lake - it seems vast - you cannot see the far shore - a strange glow – out there - white – almost blue then snow - a few flakes falling – the whole world seems altered – an otherworld - insubstantial - unreal - yet the ice at your feet is thick and hard...

...you put one foot on it – carefully – testing it - it feels stronger than the earth itself – you stamp your foot – it is solid – hard – you stamp again and again – it will not crack – you stand squarely on it – jump up and down - more solid than you can ever imagine – if you were locked in there you would never escape...

...you stare down into it - strange patterns below the surface – more flakes falling now – the glow on the ice – far out...

...good day young sir - a voice behind you – an unfamiliar accent...

...perhaps you might consider a burl about the lake...

…he is tall – stooped – arms hang loose at his side – strange yet somehow familiar…

Janet Peace

'The secret of life is enjoying the passage of time,' James Taylor

A retired educationalist Janet Peace lives near the spectacular North Coast of Northern Ireland. Writing is a comparatively new passion joyfully discovered since joining North Coast Writers. As a new hobby, writing jostles for position with tending a large, unkempt garden, fostering and caring for equally unkempt rescue cats and an old, faithful border-collie as well as dabbling in art, music and D.I.Y. interior design. Her large family, many pets, stunning location and reflections on life all inspire her poetry. Her poem 'Tapestry' featured in the Anthology *Love, Loss and Cardiac Issues,* and in *Springboards: a Manual of Creative Writing,* both published by Impspired Press in 2022. 'The Last Dance', a poem written as a tribute to Dame Deborah James, featured in Impspired online magazine No.21 and in the Impspired print edition volume 11.

Seasons Gilt

rape fields of ore **outshine** sun's aurous might

rivalling frames of **saffron** whin for height

daffodils **trumpet brass** on grassy plain

dandelion manes **rag-rug** country lane

buttercups **be-sequin** stark darkest sedge

honey bees bumble sweet **mimosa** hedge

primroses primp and pose in wooded glade

shy celandine hide amidst sorrel shade

yolk-rich chicks and **downy** ducklings scutter

round ramshackle coop   clocked close by **mother**

brood cuckoo calls   proud nature's **jewels** sing

in Botticelli awe of a Vivaldi Spring

Reflections

Looking out
across camomile lawn
over hornbeam hedge
the woman above gazes at the lough
reflecting the mood of the sky
as it has done for aeons
her mind wanders back
to a life before
lived in this same place
a spring of cuckoo calls
nuzzling   nesting   nurturing
brooding a fresh breed

time-tranced
she watches the girl
in the cottage below
traces the patterns of her life
captures snapshots
freeze frames memories
boiling brock for ducks ....
broom-butting the goat
as it browsed the roses .....
waving-on the children
loitering the lane
late for school ....

decades drift ....
the girl below
resides within
the woman above
gazing at the lough ....
reflecting
reflecting
reflect...

refl……
re………

Rock Pool

A wind-drift seed afloat and treed
tide-timed
sea-safe
skims surface tension
casting germlings

A seaweed bract wracked on crag
salt sap
bladder-trapped
fusty crustose cyst
squeezing the sac

A hermit crab upgrading pad
glop-body
unclad
scuttles scavenged shell
sizing the next

A special child sensory needs
challenged cherished
nurtured loved
scoops with hopeful hands
divines potentiality

Pansy

outside
on a balmy day
I observed pansies
collapsed   limp
hanging heads from drought
once watered   revived
they stretched upwards
turning painted faces
towards the sun

inside
in a darkened den
tiny litter runt
last-born   feeble
lay against its mother's warmth
too weak to suckle
snuggled by siblings
twitching   murmuring
replete with mothers-milk

she had wilted
I dribbled a droplet of sugar-water
into her elfin mouth
I have seen bumblebees
with drooped antenna
buzz anew
after a bubble of such nectar.
she made no buzz
ceased to mew

I swaddled her close
took her out of the dark
into golden sunshine
unwrapped she lay on my lap
sunbeams soothing her cooling
she was so beautiful   so perfect
the sweetest heart-shaped face
the tiniest of petal ears
eyes that had never seen

we sat beside the lavender
soft-scented   soothing
butterflies battled in play
honeybees browsed lupins
birdsong wafted ....
leaves quivered
all was still   peaceful

time paused ....

my Pansy faded

TAPESTRY

our frame crafted solid
love loomed large
together we wove woollen dreams
you were my warp
I your weft
when you were down
I was up
life threw the shuttle
left to right »»»»»»»»»»»»»»»»»»»»»»»»»»»»»
««««««««««««««««««««««««««««right to left
back and forth
--------------- stacking ---------------
--------------- time ---------------
--------------- lines ---------------
your warp was taut
my weft obedient to the pull
tension finely balanced
threads spun from coarse-combed yarn
were beaten in place
patterns emerged
warp distorted
tensity slacked
weft floated free
weave unpicked
thread by thread by thread
cut loose we
U N R A V E L L E D

James Simpson

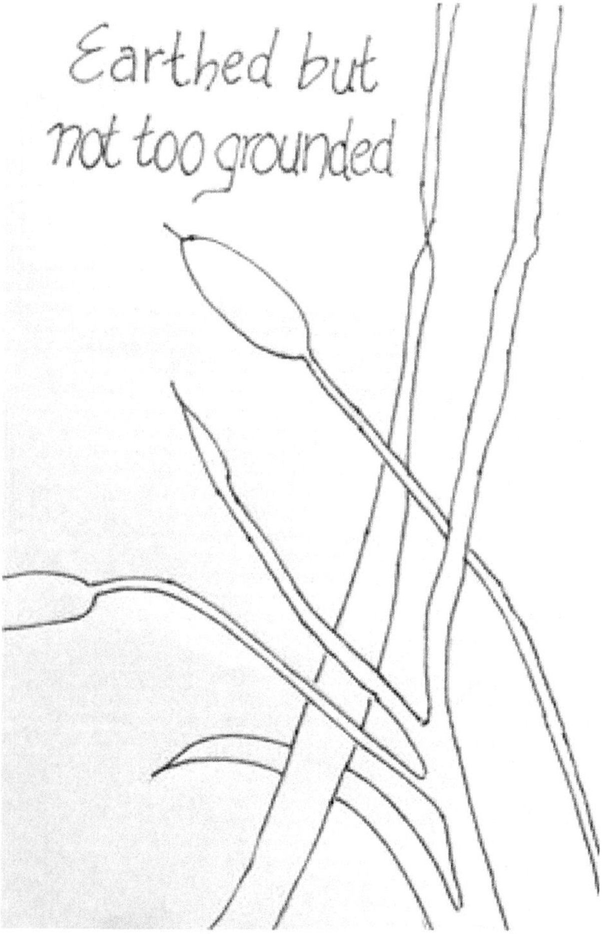

Having grown up in East Belfast, Jim Simpson was runner up in the Francis McManus Short Story Competition in 2013, and has been long listed for the RTE Guide/ Penguin Ireland award. His work is included in literary anthologies, including *On the Grass When I Arrive,'* published by Guildhall Press 2016. A winning finalist of the Irish Novel Fair in 2019, he is a graduate of The Seamus Heaney Centre, Queen's University. James, who has performed in Open Mics and given numerous readings, published *Smokes and Birds* his debut Irish Short Story collection, in 2021.*'Surprising runaway brilliance,'* Ian Sansom. He is working on a Belfast based coming-of-age novella and a humorous novel, set in Derry, the city of his adoption.

Fathers' Day

'Look after Dad,' Jim's mother had said, before she shipped to the stars, leaving Dad to Jim. Thanks Mum. 'Don't annoy Dad. Watch his bowels and narrow oesophagus.' This, minutes before blast-off, and breathed through moth-eaten lungs. Her penultimate commission, seconds before the death rattle on Ward 4.

'And rub honey on his sore place.'

Loss was loss, but to be honest, Jim breathed a sigh of—well, relief, when she got away.

So, here he was, with Dad.

'It will be better for her,' said Rev Patsy, foolishly attempting to hold Dad's hand. 'Go to hell,' Dad said. She smiled, showing halo and shiny, pink gums. 'Ah now,' she said to Jim, 'remember the fifth…'

Jim said he did. He'd done his best for Mum.

'Your job's been halved,' Patsy said foolishly, 'and on Fathers' Day.' Mum would be passing Mars now. 'Hello Red Planet.' She'd be gathering speed. Was she looking back at Jim? He didn't think so.

'Your mum's effects,' the terminal nurse had said. The one with the nose ring. Jim had shaken a little as he grasped the redundant, little bag. He'd figure out what to do with her collection of reading glasses. Maybe send them to Kenya.

Jim phoned the carers. 'We'll manage today,' he said, 'Dad and me, you know, on account of Mum.' The all-night death tax was £20. Clunk, clunk. Jim fed the parking machine. Listened to the coins drop deep, like tokens in the Amusements. Still short after £15 60, a total stranger hands him a fiver. 'Now that's compassion.' The stranger grips Jim's hand in his own dry paw. 'Been there fella,' he says, like a dealer at the mart.

'Long runs the hare,' Jim says. Words from—some meadow in his brain.

'That's right,' the stranger says, 'Good man.'

It's the in-between time. Dawn streak. First train due from the city. Jim's engine idles at the crossing. He needs organic milk for Dad. Huntley's Quality Minimart has been open since five, selling sausage baps to lorry men. The railway gates hang like guillotines. The track rods gleam, burnished by a million revolutions. World-people on wheels.

'Wakey wakey mate.' Where *is* Jim's head? He revs the Agila… First gear is stiff. Tries not to stall.

He'll fetch the Mirror for Dad, for the racing, and get him a large cream horn. 'Buy him a Fathers' Day card,' he hears Mum say. Hell no, he won't. Though she's barely cold.

'He's a bastard,' Jim tells her, now that she's gone.

He wears his comfortable jeans. The ones he'd on him that night in High Street, when he'd kissed the girl below the clock. He'd never intended—there'd been—an incident. Four policemen with truncheons. A lot of TROUBLE.

'What's he been at this time?' Good old duplicitous Dad. Always ahead of him. Always lurking behind him.

'What if he were to do it again,' Dad said, 'or something worse?' Have you thought of that Bella? Jim had stayed in the flat after that, dreaming. Slamming the bolt on the door of his north-facing room, tapping his keyboard. Venturing forth, for essentials, for Mum, and for Dad's prescriptions; his emollients, wipes and blister pills, going to the library for himself, where he also wrote his tales. Walking straight there and back. Sometimes he met Dad's girls, as Dad called them, behind time, hurrying in their pink and white, like stressed ice cream ladies. 'Hello Jim.' They stuck together.

His head was bursting with stories. The current saga was of a misfit cycling the Marianas Trench. Jim's readers will love it.

He likes a wireless in a car, does Jim. The Agila's fizzes—like a naked wire. 'Volts, volts,' he says aloud.

'How's your mum?' asks the Huntley woman with the big chest, withdrawing a little behind her till. Jim mumbles. 'Sorry for your, well you know,' she says…then brightly, 'and what about Dad?'

'Isn't he lucky, though, to have the likes of you. Would you want a card for the day that's in it?

Jim says he wouldn't.

The Mirror is depressing. Prince Andrew buying off that blond. No smoke without a blaze… how hackneyed was all that?

Death, royalty and sex unsettle Jim.

'Goodbye, Mrs Huntley.' He pulls the glass door till it scrapes. Too much aluminium in her shop. Too shabby-tinny bright.

Home. First floor. 16A Willow View. 16 B and C on either side, both vacant. 'She's gone,' he calls to dad, 'but I have your horn.' Seven o'clock. There are the pips. 'Hey Dad, I have your …'

Jim fancies a tale about Dad. He'd make him a gnome that gets thrown in a dump. Or a squashed rat on a road, if it wasn't for…stories scuttle in his head.

Dad isn't *his* Dad. He isn't anyone's, as far as Jim knows. Which is just as well for them.

'Jim's dim,' Dad had told Mum, after he married her. 'I'm a poet and I don't bloody…'

'That's droll,' Jim said to Dad.

This latest protagonist, in the Trench, is making progress at the very bottom, going at a steady ten knots on the bicycle, which is good, considering the monsters which have left it too long to surface. Jim's character has no name—as yet.

'Is that you Jim?' Dad stirring.

Jim's handy in the kitchen. Can handle bleach and knives, cook with gas and electric. He loads the kettle jug. Russell Hobbs. Arranges Dad's tray. Nescafé, two sugars, the horn and so forth. Then a name comes to the surface. *Hobbs Russell.* Not bad. He likes it. A touch of the goblin about it. Sub aqua, intrepid Hobbs.

There are six stairs in the flat that he and Mum have shared with Dad. A metallic ramp for Dad. Dad's tray has woven cane sides, and in the middle, the picture of a burly piper, black busby, sporran, kilt. Hobbs Russell hates kilts. Jim's heard him ranting more than once from the Pacific floor, about, 'Effing, women's skirts.' He'd rip them off their arses,' he says, which Jim finds quite endearing.

Dad had once been a good-looking chap, according to Mum. Jim wouldn't know. She'd liked good skin on a husband. Dad's skin is wrinkled now. Prune-man, Jim calls him. Too many baths?

'Things will be different after Mum,' the G P had said to Jim. By which he meant, 'after Mum goes sky rocketing.'

'So, she's gone?' says Dad, scrutinising the tray, like a priest scanning sins. His eyes are dry.

Hylo 40. Jim finds the dropper. 'Let *me,*' he says. 'Oh yes,' Jim says, two blobs in each of Dad's orbs. 'They gave me her hand luggage.' He'd avoided looking at the nurses directly, just in case. Maybe they read the papers.

'She's soaring now,' Jim says to Dad, 'Galactically.'

'Aye right.' Dad lies on his bed and scratches. He gave up walking, and now he can't. 'Bring us this Jim,' he says, and 'bring us that.' Jim knows he did that girl no harm. Not Jim, of all people.

Hobbs Russell has strong legs, and he needs them both. The Trench is no cake walk. But at least there are no tangled air lines, no cannulas snagged on weed. Also, Hobbs has evolved a set of gills, and perhaps is growing fins. The bike—pure tetracarbon—sails with grace, spoke-flashing aquatically, pneumatic tyres refusing to doze in the brine or puncture on razor rocks.

'You'll need to ring her Reverence,' Dad chews his horn. Squeezes out cream. 'You'll be wanting prayers?' Too late for prayers.

Dad slurps his tea. 'The News,' he says. 'What's in the News?'

'A man on a bicycle,' Jim says, 'beneath the ocean.'

Rev Patsy did the, dust to dust thing in a friable, feminine way. Dad sat there in his wheelchair, in the fresh, red graveyard muck, face polished as a hub cap, needing a smoke. A bee lands on his head. Jim let it sit.

'So much mold out of one hole,' Dad says. Mum will be nearing Venus. She'd known all about Dad. But she'd done nothing.

'Such love,' said Patsy. 'Between a man and woman.'

Hobbs Russell rode on. The water was 1 degree C, but he had rubbed whale blubber on his body. A good inch of thickness all over.

Mum had taught Jim to swim, before *Dad 1* made off for paradise. 'I loved that man,' she'd said. 'But now you have Dad 2.'

He had indeed.

Afterwards, Mrs Sinton, from over the way, joined Peter Doherty and the Crombie twins, neither of whom was anywhere near wise, and they trekked with her Reverence, Dad, (imperial in his chariot) and Jim, who was wheeling Dad, to the Bowling Hall. The Queen smiled distantly, from a wall. The names of former bowling presidents were listed on a board, beginning in 1910.

The Bennetts from downstairs did not attend, as they were in Tenerife.

'You'll be all right with Jim,' Mrs Sinton told Dad. 'He'll have nothing to do now, but look after *you*.' The twins nodded.

'God bless them,' said Reverend P, re-applying her lipstick.

Peter brought Jim a stout from a sad volunteer named Sally. 'Get it down you,' he said, 'you're going to need it.'

'She wasn't as good a woman as my first woman,' Dad told the company.

And all the while, Hobbs Russell is calling. Bubbles spewing, like spermatozoa, from his mouth. It's purple-dark below the swell, but Jim can make him out.

Hobbs is, at this very moment embracing an amphipod, chatting idly, on his break, with passing holothurians. 'Come and join me,' he mouths at Jim. Perhaps he means…but then …?

'Are there any cream horns?' Dad asks.

That night, already back on his lap top, Jim reflects on Hobbs Russell in the Marianas, and what he'd communicated. Two inter-connected messages appeared to have come from Hobbs.

Later Jim runs a bath for Dad, whose folds sag loosely on his hips. 'Just you and me,' Jim says.

'Did you add Aveeno?' Dad asks. 'Have you warmed the towel? Did you test the temperature with your elbow?

'You need two people, for the hoist.' Dad swears at Jim, but Jim holds steady. 'You'll be grand with me,' he says.

Jim cradles Dad. Makes sure he's comfortable in the saddle. Doesn't crush his bits. Lowers him in. Fluffs up the suds. Gives him his teeth. Checks he's secure. 'Comfy are you?' he asks, like any good son. Hands Dad his paper. Pulls the ring on his tin of Tenants. Dad likes a beer in the tub. Tunes the damp proofed Roberts to Classic FM. Rachmaninov. Terrific. Exuberant piano.

'Louder, louder, for God's sake,' Dad says, not thinking.

Jim smiles. 'Enjoy,' he says to Dad, like Dad deserves it. Jim stands outside the bathroom door, closes it to, out of respect. Gives Dad his place on Fathers's Day. But he does not close it tight.

'I'll be with you in ten,' he calls, 'to see how you're getting on.'

In the kitchen, Jim turns on the gas. All four rings. 'I'll roast you a chicken,' he calls to Dad, though he fails to strike a match.

Hobbs beckons.

Jim lifts his mum's terminal bag. Now it contains some Airtex Y-fronts, and a bottle of Jameson. Black and white piano notes stream madly from the bathroom. Rock a bye Dad. There'll be no one about till morning, when the carers call, 'Good morning. Hello. Good God.'

Clutching his ThinkPad, Jim leaves the flat to join Hobbs Russell, whose first message, he reflects, had included;

'Pressure too great.'

Second message, 'Get out quick. Belt and braces.'

Fathers' Day mizzle and murk. But Jim's vision is twenty/twenty. He leaves in brogues, on foot, avoiding Huntley's. With seconds to spare, he catches the 21 19, already lost in the crowd, in the jostle of sea-creatures scrambling for a seat.

Jacob's Ladder

It had started with a great idea. I would ask the men to the house. Jennifer would be on teas. Nothing elaborate. She loved to hear them sing. Dark chocolate digestives. No sitting, till the break. Standing's the thing, in a circle, listening with your whole body, to yourself and your friends, eyes smiling open windows to the music, ears tuned to the depths. That was the way. Stan sat, but Stan was on sticks. Paul J leaned on the arm of the long couch. A lot of us were old boys picking up harmonies like pebbles.

At first it went well. I'd run off a sheaf of songs for every man. A bundle each for Charles and Pete, Sean, Alan and the rest. First Number 2, then 5, and 6. Easy does it. No rush. Organised. Shuffling of paper, of singers, Tom on my right, Derek to my left, only John and Philip missing. Brian, beady behind his horn rims, bright as an owl. Highs and lows, together we climbed Jacob's ladder.

'Stand closer.' Me. 'Pretend you *like* one another.' Laughs, nudges, jostles. Huddles. 'Hold the long note.'

'Soldiers of the Cross. Thank God for the blood. Now count to four.

'Wait till we *really* know it,' I say. Layer on layer, of light and shade. What is it about men singing? In

Cornwall we'd be fishermen. In the Valleys, coalminers. What is it about leading them? The privilege of it. The soul stirring rapture. The pure, swelling ocean of it. The solemnity of a slow air, poured like a good beer. The blending balm of Gilead. 'Gently now.' Building. 'Think of it, men...to heal the sin sick soul. If you don't like *sin,* then think of pain. Of wounds being stanched. Open the vowel. We don't sing *bam, jam* or *ham*. Lengthen it. *Balm,* that's it, not *bomb*. Imagine a knife slash dressed with ointment, of salve on raw flesh on the road to Jericho, of a stranger's generous oil.'

Paul Robson's curls spin now at thirty-three and a third RPMs as I hear my dad in the long ago. 'What a bass voice Jim.' The orchestra followed Robson as he made the time his own, varied the pace, moved it along—didn't drag, '...He died to save us all. Yes, lengthen the *All,* draw it out, like a trombone slide, hold it, hold it… wait till the tenor kicks in. But not too long. Not long enough to murder it.' No piano. We go it alone, acapella. 'Think of the meaning. Back down for the refrain. Lighter. Lighter. Ah yes, the words…'

The best ever.

One more, before the break. All My Trials. The Joan Baez song. 'I have a little book, rhyme it with brook,' don't flatten it, '… pages three and every page spells—liberty.' That's good. That's right.

'If living were a thing ....' We need to give it more air guys, more urgency, '...the rich would live'—a tiny pause—'and the poor, rounded lips for the poor, step it down, tenderly now. 'All my trials—can you feel the weariness, can you get the resignation, the deep despair, and yet the relief. Life in the ghetto, guys, will soon be over.'

'Too late my brother...'

A sudden gear shift.

Tyre scorch and smoke. The room spins. No air. Open a door. A window. All the windows. The pressure's in my head. My head is cooking. Steaming. My head's a cabbage. Hair's a river. Shrill, shrill train whistle in my brain. Alarm sounds. Alarm. Legs wobble. Moisture drips clots. I'm sopping. Need a sponge. Steam building. Needle rising.

Jennifer has brewed the tea. She hands around mugs. A few with sugar. The splash of milk.

Sweat rolling.

Roiling.

I'm tholing. Not saying.

Thawing

Boiling

Thawing.

Skin plastered scalp-melt.

A dam bursts in my head.

'I need a drink.' I'm in the kitchen, standing on the old beige tiles, grasping a long, desperate glass of cold water. I'm palm-clutching, finger-gripping. Gulping. Holding onto the island from Ikea, clinging to the self-assembled altar, steadying, mumbling.

Am I all right?

'No, I'm not myself,' I tell Jennifer. The lads are bubbling. There's craic and there's me, not wanting to make a fuss. But a sledge hammer pounds my brow, panel beating, skull metal working. A slab shifts. A riveting, shipyard din of black smoke chokes me, and oh, it's—stretching, stretching me. Thunder rumbles. Neck, stiff as a brace, two hundredweight of coal lumps on my shoulders. I'm sipping. Slipping. No warning. Pneumatic. The floor falls away. Slime slathers. I've no notion yet of the spillage, of the overflow splatter, the breach in the cistern.

I'm back in the room with the lads, astride a yellow, polypropylene chair. 'I'm grand,' I say. But I'm not grand. We begin again. I want to, want to, but I can't—sing, because I can't stand, and the mountain is on me. Smothering.

I give in. 'Another time.' The guys leave in twos and threes, low voices wish me the best.

'He's pale.'

Heads shake.

'He's a shocking colour.'

'A ghost.' They hope it's nothing.

'It's the heat.'

'It's a warm night.'—For January.

They hesitate, linger, the way you do. Marvel at the filament-snap fragility, the suddenness. Paul phones Phyllis. 'Darling, I need a lift. No, please come now.' Under the slick I'm feeling their care, as the vice tightens and the Grey Fella grips me tighter in his teeth, clutching me in obscene pink paws, to screw me, like a lemon, till I squeak, scrunging me in his juicer. Revolving, ripping. Wringing me till I spew.

'I'll be fine. Need to lie down. Flat. Yes flat.' Somehow, upstairs I'm in bed. If I can just…',

But Jennifer says, 'No.'

She drives. I loll in the passenger seat. Red lights. I stand at the window in A and E. 'Name?' asks the clerk.

'Fierce headache,' I say. 'The worst.'

'Address. D.O.B.? Take a seat.' I take a seat. I sprawl across two seats. Can't sit up straight. The pain. A man I know. Another Jim. 'Is Jim ok?'

Jim's not ok.

The triage room. The nurse. I need to throw up. Throw up in a bin.

I slump some more.

A doctor. 'The pain. On a scale of one to ten?'

Language. Calibration. One to ten? 'Eight,' I say, trying. 'Or nine.' How does nine sound? 'What is ten like?'

The scan result.

'You've had a bleed. 'Subarachnoid.' Imagine, my very own, eight-legged, underground, spider-monster, huge, red and oozing. 'I've heard of it,' I say.

A race across the Sperrins, trolleyed, trussed, strung out, but not out cold, in the small chilly hours of a dark, thin morning, yet a glimmer inside the van. Strange, but cosy as a snug. A private pub capsule on the move. Without the beer. No windows? 'Drip-fed paracetamol through a cannula, from a polythene bag, suspended at a height, from a hook. Ebbs into me through a plastic tube. I think of goldfish. The para medic reads something. I don't know what. Scant traffic. 'No need to blue light.' The driver is a woman.

'We're off,' she says, addressing me, I think, in a green looking boilersuit, like a spotless car mechanic, all energy, ready to sink the shoe, as she clamps doors shut. Metal on hermetic metal. The road to Dungiven. Engine throb, tyres burn through Glenshane, past the Ponderosa, hell bent for The Royal, past Jamesie's, down the M2, ahead of the Grey Fella, heart beating to the drum, to the thrum of the road. The songs we sang are on a loop. Jacob is up and down his ladder a thousand times, up, up—head-tumbling credits scroll empty popcorn in my mind.

A blank. Where am I? I'm dozing, at the end of the line, as we swish to a halt. The handbrake jerk. The engine cuts. The R V H, where my sister trained in the seventies when bullets flew. When she lay on the floor of Bostock House, with her head down. When provos and police were filled with lead.

White light. Space. I'm on the move. Porters. I'm fading. Trundling. At the end of the beginning. The beginning of becoming a patient in Neurosurgery. Where I'd visited my friend Wes—what was it, only months ago—after they removed his tumour. It had taken nine hours.

Sue Steging

Sue Steging was born in Liverpool. She now lives by a river, surrounded by trees and within easy reach of the sea. After a career spanning education and psychotherapy she is glad to have found time to observe and write about the world around her and grateful for the support of family, friends and local writers in pursuing this new interest. Sue's work has been published in journals and anthologies and was longlisted for the Seamus Heaney Award for New Writing in 2021 and 2022.

a naming of parts

a feather falls from flight
light, down-soft, quill-sharp
entry to imagined worlds and spaces
where secret geometries of flight
invisible unities of form and function
gesture toward
planetary arcs
an orbital ellipse
a universe in motion

pearl edges undulate
like waves from deeper, greyer seas

fine edges of a basin so shallow
an age might ache for the arc of its circumference to meet
itself
a movement so slow
so careless of a pattern hungry eye

there is violence in labels   a fumbling assault

to classify and catalogue
the shaft - the vanes - the downy barbs
disrupts these silent harmonies of air
synchronies
I thumbed open with desire

the day I tried to know and name the parts

Spiders

The track was flanked by spiders overnight.
It looks as though a phalanx came,
deployed their sheet traps dense and flat
energising funnel twists
like those parabolas we build
to catch the sound behind the light.

We love to see the bracken dressed
in sparkling, sequinned tulle
but that's not why the spiders came.
The sticky, labyrinthine silks will
ambush falling flyers, creepers-by
or hang unseen to snare and scare us
in the dark while we revert to atavistic spite.

As we tune in to signals
sourced beyond our sun,
do we transmit the screams
and sighs of predators and prey?
If there are listeners farther out
I hope they never hear
the man who bartered for
a starving woman's child.
His money-web has bound a wife
to larder for his son.

Antiphony

words wound
  a knife draws scars that dare not fade

    words shimmer
      bright rainbows shoal through coral sharps

words wander
  a parent who abandons leaves wondering in their wake

    words float
      still waters mirror crystals laid down deep

words skewer
  a spike pins you close when you had hoped to leave

    words hover
      hope draws an apparition in the mist

words stifle
  a voice calls out secrets that were only yours to tell

    words wait
      it's time to sing your part

bonfire

before
midday
tolls equinox
the latest
summer prunings
join the pyre
long
lavender stems
transform
in the
magic of
cremation
embers writhe
sublime
leave their ashy
trace in
food
for future
selves
while
small leaves spin
copper
from the sky
paper pennies
the beech
deposits
summer's last largesse

At Knockoneill Court Tomb

grass moths startle   stirred   by our crossing

a tussocked boundary

stumble stones

we surrender to not knowing   what belongs   to then

to them   these builders   interring just one human
perhaps   with so much care

unknowing   that   peat   would come   make its
own arrangements   burying
foundations   grave goods
smothering cultures
under fallen greens   the deaths of trees

today   save   a few plantations   here and there   the
hills are bare   they make an arc   a shelter

offer rocky embrace   to a memorial
          aligned   now   with a stand of steely turbines

while lichen sets its own   slow   circles on the stone

mesmerised by rotation

          we meditate on the future

     as our forerunners

          might have wondered

               what their dead

would see

                    through a grass moth's eyes

Rhona Stephens

Born and raised in Northern Ireland, Rhona Stephens has lived at various times in each of the four nations of the United Kingdom. She currently divides her time between Scotland's Royal Deeside and Ireland's Causeway Coast. Books have been her treasured companions on life's pilgrimage. In North Coast Writers, she has found fellow travellers who share her delight in unveiling the power, potential and pleasures of the written word. Her work has appeared in *Irish Hares and Seahorses,* and in *Love, Loss and Cardiac Issues,* both Anthologies published by Impspired Press in 2022. Her children's poems have appeared on *The Dirigible Balloon* and *Charles Causley Trust* websites.

Refresh

On days when
leaves lie limp
and birds lie low
when globes of
silver lichen swell
on darkened twigs and
moss-wrapped stumps
glow alien green;
when tussocked grass
close-curled below
bows so
raindrop gems
slow slip-slide
down the
stooping
stems
down
down
to safely land on softened ground
when puddles grow and earth
cold-pressed by drumming rain
exhales - a peaty breath
scenting air
and skin
and hair
and trees

on days like these
  come see how
    the woods
      refresh

Return rose-pink in cheek and nose
hair silver-sprinkled mizzle-moist
toes tingle-teased by nips of cold
chilled hands precurled
to close-wrap cups of
steaming liquid gold
        return
heart   strong
lungs   cleared
mind   calm
soul   cheered

        Come
come to the woods

        Refresh

Survivor

When I see you
when I see you with your sisters
in the store
a subtropical citrus
transported from your native soil
marked down to a quarter of your worth
when I see you
abandoned
on a shabby clearance trolley
pale
frail
parched
leaves
clinging
to a brittle stem
scarce breathing
When I see you
I cannot leave without you

And so we begin
you and me
a cautious relationship
you a dilatory patient
me an impatient consultant
of Google
where I learn that
you are susceptible to
root-rot
frost

And aphids

You survive
roots ✔ strong
trunk ✔ sturdy
leaves ✔ sleek
fruit ✔ sweet-sharp
cheerful ovals

I like to think you are content
and yet
when I see you
when I see you reach
for our timid northern sun
or struggle to escape
the generous pot
that binds you in my world
I wonder

I wonder if
some silent memory cell
stirs a longing for home
I wonder if you miss
the freedom to explore
on a whim
to stretch your roots
I wonder if you dream of
rain tip-tapping on your leaves
half-remembered melodies
whispered songs of sweet communion
with your kind

Greeting

she is perfect
nascent beauty
in a body ivory smooth butter soft
lash and brow sweet shadows on her lovely face
hair - a dusting -
midnight dark
and ears
mirrored perfection
formed within me - within *me*
close-curled fingers
toes a marvel of artistry
and lips parting pouting
to cry
or to suckle strong against my breast
I hold her kiss-close
surely
surely that is a whisper of breath
a first whisper against my cheek
for she is perfect!

no they say
her heart…
not possible to detect in utero…
nothing they could do…nothing I have done…
they're sorry…I'm sorry…
…not my fault they say again
and again…
and yet

I feel the need to apologise to her
again and
again and
again…
  I'm sorry…

where will my love
my words
my dreams
stored up for you
where will they go?
what shall I do with them?
stored nine months three days
No!
stored a lifetime
for I thought of you
twenty years ago
on Christmas Day when
I hugged the softness
smelt the sweetness
soothed the sadness
of my new baby doll
who did not breathe
but as I held her
was alive to me
as you are now

where will they go these sorrows
these tears for you who will
never cry
nor smile
nor laugh for the joy
of being alive
Oh… what shall I do with my tears
when the acceptable season of grief is past?

I am lost in the astonishment of grief
the slipperiness of a sorrow
that can't be
captured
contained
controlled
a sorrow with a beginning
but in this pre-dawn world
no end

When the rain gets warmer

Excepting the highest of tides and most severe of storms, I walk the beach every morning. Most of the year, my companions are local people, all of whom I know by name, many of whom I count as friends. Occasionally, two or three of us walk together. For the most part, however, we respect each other's unspoken desire for a solitary start to the day.

Summer brings change to our routines. Come the longer days, come the tourists, so we rise earlier and walk earlier. By and large, the holidaymakers do what holidaymakers do everywhere. Many enjoy a leisurely breakfast before heading to the beach to walk off the effects of an Ulster fry. A handful, spurning a lie-in, rise early enough to walk the beach alongside the locals.

Beach-walking holidaymakers tend to be strollers rather than striders, allowing multiple opportunities for eye contact and conversation. But the young woman who joined us every morning last week left neither room nor breath for conversation, for she strode across the strand at a speed that left many of us locals behind. All the more surprising, as she was pushing a special needs buggy.

I saw compassion in the eyes of everyone who glanced her way. Perhaps that is what she wished to avoid, for she kept her gaze fixed on the pier as she walked away from the promenade; then, on the return lap, focused resolutely on the monument crowning the hill that sheltered us from the worst of the westerlies.

There was resolution in more than this young woman's eyes, and it spoke of something beyond a determination to keep fit. Still in her thirties, I guessed, her face had a maturity beyond her years. The strength of her profile, her steady gaze and the set of her shoulders told a tale of self-sufficiency, of survival. Of having been tried and tested and come forth as gold from a furnace. I surmised this was related to and bound up with that young life reclining in the buggy.

During the early part of last week, I met the young woman as I made my return along the beach. But on Wednesday, arriving later than usual, I was about five metres behind her as we set off from the promenade. By the time we doubled back for the return, she had increased that gap by some distance.

We were about halfway along the beach when it happened. Eyes fixed on the monument, the young woman failed to notice a black bag slip from the parcel tray under the buggy onto the sand. I increased my pace, for the tide was incoming and already a couple of waves had nudged the tideline well beyond the bag. But the half-dozen incoming waves that lapped the shore before I reached the bag restrained themselves, for it was untouched by anything save the damp sand.

I held it close, set off and tried to gain on the young woman. No easy challenge, for she had the longer stride and the advantage of about thirty years less mileage on her body clock.

At last, I got close enough to call out.

"Excuse me."

She turned, with more wariness than welcome in her eyes.

"You dropped this," I panted. "Or rather, it fell out of the buggy."

"Ohhhh." She laid a hand over her mouth. "Thank you."

Having secured the bag in the parcel tray, she turned to face me again.

There followed an awkward moment when we were without words and without certainty as to what to do next. Finally, I motioned for her to go ahead.

"I'm afraid I couldn't match your pace," I smiled.

She caught hold of the buggy and seemed about to resume her walk. Then she turned back.

"Shall we walk together?"

I smiled up at her. "So long as you cut your speed."

She laughed as I fell into step beside her.

"I'm very grateful to you," she said. "That bag contains Joshua's medication. We can't go anywhere without it and if he needed it…"

She said no more, but in my mind I completed that sentence for her.

"Glad I noticed it, then. I'm Susie, by the way. Susie Wilson. I live just off Sea Road."

"Do you come here every morning?"

I nodded. "This morning, I overslept, so I'm a bit later than usual."

I paused, leaving room for her to speak, but she said nothing.

"What about you?" I asked, as the silence lengthened. "Are you on holiday? Or have you moved to the area?"

"We're staying in the village for a week's holiday."

Arriving at the boardwalk, she turned the buggy round and, pulling it behind her, made her way up to the promenade.

Following her, I found myself at eye level with Joshua. He was perhaps seven or eight years old and shared his mother's steady gaze. But the engagement that brought her eyes to life was absent in her son. Beneath a coronet of curls, his little face showed little evidence of understanding or interest in what was going on.

Back on level ground again, the young woman repositioned the buggy in front of her.

"I'm going this way," she said.

"And I'm heading in the opposite direction."

So we parted. Only as I walked away from the promenade did I realise she had not even told me her name.

****

Next morning, as I made my way to the beach at the usual time, I was surprised to see her already on the promenade. She waved and pushed the buggy towards me.

"Going for your walk?"

I nodded.

"Mind if I join you?"

"I'd be delighted," I said, hoping the surprise did not show on my face.

So we set off. At my pace.

By the time the walk was nearing an end, our conversation had ranged from craft shops to climate change, jellyfish to jambalaya. She was an interesting and interested companion, who spoke easily and listened attentively. But after half an hour in her company, all she had shared about herself was that her name was Naomi and she had moved some months ago from the city to work in the local hospital.

As we were leaving the beach, a minibus pulled in and parked in front of us. The rear doors opened and a spill of youngsters, bursting with life and laughter, jostled onto the pavement. The group gave every indication of staying put for some time, unpacking bags and beach balls, surfboards and wetsuits in no particular order, and with no particular haste.

I glanced towards Naomi, intending to ask if we should cross to the other side of the road. But the expression on her face stole my words, stole my breath. A look of such yearning flowed across her face as prompted me to drop my gaze. It was too personal, too raw to observe.

Like a flock of birds, the youngsters suddenly dispersed, flying past us with a collective whoop. Naomi turned to watch them, following their progress down the boardwalk until they disappeared from view behind a sand dune. As she turned back, she looked down at the buggy for a moment before moving forward. I felt I learnt more about her in those few minutes than I could have discovered in a week of conversation.

Before going our separate ways, we agreed to meet the following morning when again conversation flowed. Initially, at least. I sensed Naomi had something on her mind, so allowed our chat to dwindle to a natural close. We walked in silence for a while.

One disadvantage of a beach walk is a potential encounter with dog walkers who let their pets roam too freely. A few dogs had already made over-enthusiastic approaches to Joshua before being called back by their owners. Turning to ask Naomi if he was frightened of animals, I noticed a tear on her cheek.

"Just a grain of sand," she said, dismissing my concern. "Or the wind." She wiped away another tear.

Sympathy cures no ills and pays no bills, my father used to say, so for a while I said nothing. Eventually, I asked what I thought was the most innocuous of questions.

"Have you enjoyed your week by the sea?"

Shutting her eyes, Naomi drank in the salty air before replying.

"It's been wonderful." She opened her eyes and looked at me. "I've got more annual leave to take and I was hoping I could get accommodation for next week, too. But… I had a call just before I came out. There's nothing."

"It's been… *wonderful*,' she repeated, leaning on the word as if it were her life-support. "Wonderful to get away from the flat. And the bleeper."

As she came to a standstill, I turned towards her. Another tear dampened her lashes. I felt sure it had nothing at all to do with the wind or the sand.

"Joshua hates the flat. And there's a limit to how many walks you can take in one day. It's…"

Then she raised a hand, shook her head as if to dispel a train of thought. "It's not your problem. I'm so sorry."

I laid a hand on her arm. "Let's walk," I said, remembering my father's words.

But I remembered, too, what we had read together at our church service on Sunday. *Bear one another's burdens*. So, I tentatively asked a few questions. And Naomi quietly gave a few answers.

By the time we reached the pier, she had told me about Joshua's birth, that he had a genetic illness, that her husband left when Joshua was just five months old.

By the time our walk was over, the tears were gone, self-composure restored. I was not surprised when my invitation to join me for a coffee was turned down. She had to go. Make a few calls. Attend to Joshua. But she thanked me. Very much.

"See you tomorrow?" I asked.

"I don't think I can make it. I have to check out by ten o'clock."

"We could meet after that, if you like," I said. "I'll leave it up to you."

"Well, if you don't mind going later," she said, as I turned to go. "That would be great."

We agreed that Naomi would pack the car, return the key and meet me on the promenade at a quarter past ten on Saturday morning.

****

"Looks like there's rain on the way." I nodded towards Innishowen.

"Really?"

Naomi looked surprised and I knew why. Overhead, the sky was clear, the sun warm. But I had lived long enough in the village and listened often enough to the locals to read the skies over Donegal. There would be rain. And since neither of us had a jacket, we had better hurry or risk getting caught in it.

We almost made it. Backs to the sea, we were heading up to the boardwalk when the rain arrived. It did not take time to introduce itself, bursting upon us, puffing and pitting the soft sand as we made our way up the beach.

"At least it's summer rain," I said, when we made it to the shelter, just as the rain eased off.

"There's a difference?" Naomi asked.

"Well, they say, *It's summer in Ireland when the rain gets warmer.*"

She looked at me and laughed. "Small mercies then."

We tried to dry ourselves with a muslin cloth Naomi had in her bag and a summer scarf I had in my pocket.

"This is hopeless," I said, as droplets continued to trickle down my neck. "Come back to my house. We can dry out properly over a cup of tea or coffee."

For a moment, I thought she would accept the invitation, then the shutters fell, her self-containment returned.

"No, no, we'll be fine," she said. "It won't take long to get back to the flat. Joshua gets agitated in strange places. Besides, it's tricky getting the buggy in and out of other people's houses."

I could not let this pass. It felt as if the moment had been prepared for me, the opportunity presented to me.

"My father-in-law lived with us for several years after he had a stroke, Naomi. I have level entry to my house. And accessible rooms. Do come," I urged.

And to my surprise, she did.

****

Hands wrapped round a cup of tea, I sat at my kitchen table. Opposite, wrapped in my old dressing gown, Naomi sipped her coffee, all the while keeping an eye on Joshua. We had settled him beside the open patio doors, where he could watch the wind bring leaves to life and see the shadows filter through to dance across the lawn.

Naomi took a long slow breath. "It's soooo peaceful."

I took a sip of tea before responding.

"You'd be very welcome to stay here this coming week, Naomi. You've seen the house, you've seen the rooms, so you know it would work."

"That's very kind, Susie. And you're right, it would work fine for Joshua. But I can't impose on you further. It's time I got our things together and left you in peace."

She drained her coffee cup and took it to the sink.

I stirred my tea, tapped the teaspoon on the rim of the cup and laid it on the table. Considering what I might say, I felt my shoulders tense, for it is not in my nature to challenge anyone.

"I think that's your head speaking, Naomi. I think your heart is whispering it would be better for Joshua to be here than back in the flat. And I think you would love another week by the sea, too, before going back to work."

With perfect timing, Joshua gave a low slow call that blossomed into a chuckle of delight.

Our heads turned towards him. His little face transformed by a smile, he was watching a blackbird cock its head one way, then the other, before dipping to bathe in the bird bath at the edge of the patio.

"That's the first time I've heard Joshua laugh." I smiled, turning to look at his mother again. "Listen to your heart, Naomi. Listen to my heart. I would love you both to stay."

I watched her watching her son as the blackbird continued to entertain him. It seemed a long time before she came back and sat opposite me again.

"Are you sure?"

I nodded. "Absolutely sure."

"I seem to have spent most of the week thanking you for one thing after another, Susie. I really appreciate this. More than I can say. You've brought… You've brought summer to our lives this week."

I pointed to our dressing gowns. "It hasn't been all sunshine."

"No," Naomi agreed. "But you know it's summer when the rain gets warmer."

Our eyes met and we turned to look at Joshua. We both knew she was not talking about the weather.

Ian Turnbull

Retired in Northern Ireland, Ian has been published in periodicals in both the US and the UK. He also devises improvised comedy sketches which are not scripted. He wrote scripts for videos whilst working for a television company, but it was on accounting. He is inspired by Christianity, where he lives and anything that isn't accounting. His poem *The Truth* was published in the Anthology *Love, Loss and Cardiac Issues,* Impspired Press, 2022

The Truth

The truth is what has been, what is and what will be
    it is the heart of the matter

it is not defeated by our memories or desires
    it is not compromised by our dealings

it has a singular purity
    in a sea of plural deceit

it is as much a stranger on the statements of those who would rob the rich
    as it is on the tax returns of the rich who would rob the poor

there are many who pay lip service to it and give it no value
    those who do value it hold on to it for all they are worth.

The Blasted Tree

look at my might
howled the wind
see the tree
not a branch stands upright
each points the way I go
I have prevailed
it bows to my will

the
tree
letting the wind
have its way
stays defiant
for no matter
how many times
bowed by hard blows
it still stands

Exposure

~ Inspired by Act 3 Scene 2 of King Lear
by William Shakespeare ~

How say you who is the fool

Unheeded only Cordelia was true

Ruthless truthless two other daughters have I

Relentless roofless the winds and rain scour

I am as blind as my good ally Gloucester gouged

Crack crack the storm heralds my kingdom rent

Am I a man more sinned against than sinning

Nonsense is now my court

Only the jester remains

Egotist my judgement received

Sorrows my true worth

Speaking Volumes

~ One and Two ~

Used and Abused

Ruddy marvellous. Years of service, what do I end up with? A broken spine and they still expect me to perform. No rest for the wicked. Others get proper treatment. Everything put back the way it should be. Not me. I got the bloke who thought he knew what he was doing. I know what it's like to be under the knife. It was Friday afternoon and it was a Friday afternoon job. I reckon he had beer on his breath. I was patched up and put straight back out there.

I wouldn't mind, but they can't even pronounce my name right over here. I'm on the shelf, treated like I belong in another era. Last Saturday, a bloke, rough as a badger's back-side, came in to check me out. *Let's find out what Rod Jet can tell us about "thoroughfare"*. Slapped me right on my back as well. It's French, you idiot, Roget, *Rozh ay*, you fool, ass, donkey, cretin, moron, imbecile…

Reunited

One in the afternoon and John was bleary eyed from staring at his computer. People couldn't even act on advice by phone now. Too lazy to make their own notes, *oh could you email me that?*

Lunchtime meant getting away from the screen, getting hold of the stuff he loved. Books were a safe haven. Poetry was his real thrill. Relaxing with a bit of Shelley or some Coleridge could pass a few hours.

His ex had wanted one of the handmade oak bookcases. She'd cleared many prized volumes off to an unnamed charity shop, to free up that piece of furniture. *Well, you've read them all anyway,* was her explanation. That action had left him more bereft than being thrown out of the marital home.

David's bookshop, a favourite haunt, was now in view. That, and a few other second hand book emporiums, were helping him restore his collection.

Low tables in front of the hallowed ground carried paperbacks and hardbacks. Spines pointing toward the sky, you could lean over and make your selection. His eyes were drawn to the second row. There it was right in front of him, a familiar slim green volume. It had an even more familiar tear in the dust jacket, some yellowing

Sellotape stopped the tear. Bought at the book launch, the author had scribbled in a special message for him. He snapped open the cover. It was his copy. With great joy he read the words, *Now piss off and don't bother me again! Frank.*

Mary Farrell

Facilitator of three Writing groups in Northern Ireland, North Coast Writers, Words Inc and Sanderlings, and the online Creative Writing Facilitator for Impspired.com. Mary Farrell has been writing for five years - some poetry but she prefers writing short stories and Flash Fiction, particularly about human dynamics. Her first Collections *'It's like Walking a Tightrope'* and *'Out of the Chrysalis'* were published in 2021 and 2022. Her debut Collection of short stories, *'The Kingdom'* and *'Springboards: a Manual of Creative Writing for beginners through to facilitators'* were published in October, 2022, all four books by Impspired Press. She has had various pieces of Prose and Poetry published in Magazines and Anthologies, both locally and internationally.

Just stop…think!

Loretta bit her lip…painfully. It was becoming harder and harder to say nothing. She'd known Desiree for so long, since their first day together at Rokewold Infants to be precise. Okay, they'd not been close after Desiree moved to a different District when she married, but it was beginning to seem it would be impossible to sustain any degree of friendship with her in the future. When had she become so self-centred, so unaware of the chaos and cruelty she was strewing round her every time she opened her mouth? School Reunions had their ups and down, everyone knew that. The 32nd Annual Reunion in the Assembly Hall of Southbank High was not expected to be any different, but no-one could have predicted this level of devastation. And all because of the unstoppable stream of comments from just one person.

- I hear he left you. And for a barmaid with three kids. Tracey, you know you're all so much better off without him!

- Irwin honey, your Mama was bed-ridden for so long, you should be glad she's not suffering any more.

- College isn't for everyone, I always say. If that boy of yours feels he'll get more outta back-packing round the world, then Sherie, good for him.

- Now Nelson, don't you fret that your company's

starting to lay off workers. You'll always get another job, you're not that old yet.

And it went on… and on… and on! As she moved round the room chatting loudly to her old classmates, she left them scarred, wounded, bleeding internally. Something had to be done. Loretta waited for the right moment, then grabbed Desiree by the arm just as she was about to move onto another victim. Frogmarching her out of the Assembly Hall, she bustled them both into a nearby Science Classroom. Hands on her hips she launched into an angry tirade, about discretion and empathy, about understanding and kindness, about all the remarks Desiree should never have made, about how she should have stopped and thought before she spoke.

Eventually she ran out of steam. She stopped ranting and looked at Desiree to see if any of what she had said had registered. She was bewildered by what she saw. Desiree seemed to have shrunk, her shoulders were bowed, her lips trembling. At the same instant, both decided to sit, sinking onto a nearby graffiti-ed chipped lab bench.

Well, have you anything to say for yourself?

Desiree reached up her sleeve, pulling out a tissue. It took two false starts before she could speak.

I didn't realise, truly I didn't. I haven't seen everyone in so long. You all must have noticed I've not been to a Reunion for three years now. I…I…I just couldn't face you all. Things have gone so wrong. Steve walked out, another woman. Then two months later Mama passed. The following May my baby boy, my Lewis, decided he'd move to the Coast to get a job near somewhere he could surf at the weekends. And then the house was empty, far too big for just me. Not that it mattered in the end, I couldn't keep up the payments on a house that size by myself anyway. It had to go. And when the Wilsons retired and closed their bakery, I lost my wages from there . Got a new job as a live-in housekeeper on the other side of the river. I live there now in a flat over the garage. I thought that, as I knew what it felt like to go through these things, I could encourage everyone, show them they weren't alone. If I can keep going day after day, they can too. But it's been hard Loretta, so so hard! I know that better than most! I was just trying to…..

…and with that, she broke down completely, trying to wipe away tears with a tissue now far too damp to absorb any more moisture.

Loretta was stunned. She hadn't known any of this. She realised she hadn't registered that Desiree had not been at the last three Reunions. She hadn't known about Steve leaving. Like all her friends she'd complained when the Wilson bakery downtown had closed two years ago. Where would she get such delicious cakes in the future, not to mention their beautiful French loaves? It hadn't occurred to her to think about any staff they might have employed. She never drove through the District Desiree had moved to, would never have seen a For Sale sign, nor looked at the Obituary Notices from the local Churches.

But worse, she realised she hadn't tried to know. She had simply forgotten all about Desiree, who'd played no part in her busy social world of family, work, the Church at weekends. She'd let her slip through the slats of her life.

Kintsukuroi unmastered

~ the art of fixing broken pottery, usually with gold ~

She'd really tried. She had! *I never loved her…only you,* he'd bleated, finally realising she was going to leave him. And it was probably true, she'd thought ruefully. But a realization which covered too little, came too late. She'd tried… but despite the white heat of first couplings, the molten gold of her compassion, the blood-shot embers of their clinkered love, she couldn't make it work, not even for the twins' sake. Cases in the boot, children with her parents, her rings obsolete on his bedside table. She drove away without a backward glance, unbroken.

hearth matters

the Cottage snivelled

as it remembered

there had been trilling laughs and dancing feet, the swirls and curls of toddlers tumbling
smells of yeast and crusts, savouries and sweet crumbles, beer a-hopping and mint-sharp teas
just-birthed lambs, crook-eared sheepdogs, ancient cats curled tight on the hearthstones
with love flowing tween souls sealed by kiss-warm hugs, sweet caresses and tight holdings

the Cottage wept deep sobs

as it remembered

there had been such pain with the fire, as beams broke wide and rafters crashed
furniture withered, flame veined curtains, lino globbed in tiny pustules
photos blacked out of memory, precious carvings dissolved, keepsakes melted
and the next days dawn crept low over skeleton walls, charred ruins and the sharp taste of ash

the Cottage healed slowly

as it remembered

after the clearance the first smudge of green in the grave-
brown earth, grassroots regrown
birds quested worms in the trenches upturned and
micelings sniffed and snuffled for seeds
lichen smoothed green the stumps of foundations, moss
ironed out cracks in walls heat-blown
and the next Spring brought colour and cubs, fur babies
and new birthed, all in Natures rebound

and life thrived and continued,
continued and thrived

as life always must

Magpie left

She'd left him. Why?
He hadn't seen it coming.
He'd fashioned a nest of her favourite colours, textures, sensations. The flat was redecorated, IKEA raided for sprigs and baubles, cushions and bedding, all to her liking. Gluten-free packets in the cupboards, organic veg in the fridge. He'd swollen large with her delight when they'd bought the disco ball together, giddy with laughter at its tackiness. She'd giggled and swayed and shimmied that night, with silver lights dancing off her blue-black hair. He'd thought they'd mated for life. On Solstice Eve, he came home from work, his armful of sunflowers, and found her note.
I have to go. Goodbye.
Time stopped as the Earth jolted, then resurged but with such a slow crawl. The Longest Day became the longest day. For months, years afterwards, he haunted her familiar lairs, hovering low with a heavyweight heart.

She was gone.

He was alone.

Breached

~ (s)He came in through the bathroom window, the Beatles, 1969 ~

The Colonel watched him on the security monitor, sidling along the wall, ducking behind bushes, assuming he was invisible. Slender body, black-clad, sinister balaclava, silent sneakers. He edged ever closer to the house until he disappeared from view below the CCTV camera beside the window of a second-floor bathroom. The Colonel, straight-backed, lifted a revolver from a dresser drawer in his bedroom, and with a firm step went to wait beside the bathroom door, the only exit from that particular bathroom. The others were all ensuite.

And then he waited. He knew well how to stand motionless, had done so in many battle zones throughout his career. As he counted away the seconds, then the minutes, waiting for the burglar to ease open the door, he grew calmer and more resolute. No-one was going to invade his home, breach his defences.

The handle began to drop by millimetres, making no sound. A door gap widened in just the same way and a tiny silhouette slithered through onto the landing. The Colonel, behind a large palm plant, allowed the figure to take three paces away from him before barking out, *Stop right there or I'll shoot.* Even he was surprised at how much satisfaction there was in the theatricality of the phrase.

The figure stopped. It only took seconds for all poise and grace to melt away, the shoulders to slump and the torso to curve as if in reaction to a solar plexus punch. The Colonel, flooded with the first surging of adrenaline, was disconcerted. What to do now? Frogmarch the villain down to the hallway and phone the Police? But first things first. *Take off that mask and turn around!*

And that's when everything changed.

As a shaking hand pulled off the balaclava, a black ponytail uncoiled. A blanched face, oval eyes brimming with tears, looked up at him, lower lip trembling. She tried to speak but could only stammer *Ple…ple…please.* Disconcerted before, the Colonel was now thrown totally off-guard. He had been prepared to stare down a thug, intent on robbery, but found it difficult to keep waving a gun at this tiny slip of a girl, who was obviously terrified. *Walk in front of me, down the stairs to the hall, and no funny business!* Somehow this time, the crime drama scripting failed to ring true. He just felt uncomfortable, as if he was bullying a child who needed help.

Once in the hall, with the gun he motioned her to a chair beside the telephone table. Of course he had a mobile, it *was* the twenty-first century! but he'd always been reluctant to dispense with the landline in the hallway. *Before I call the Police, give me your story so that I know what to say to them.* That came out all wrong, he realized immediately. He should be calling the Police first. What did it matter what her story was? Why was he even asking? Perhaps it was the surprise of finding a *She* when he'd expected a *He.*

In a child's voice, little above a whisper, a tale was told. Of an invalid mother, a father long since rotting in his grave, and of her only sibling, an elder brother, just four months out of Pentonville, back home to threaten and bully. He studied Council Tax Data to register any pensioners who lived alone. He'd a mate in the Town Hall, see, who had access to such restricted information. Then he'd case houses in the Riverside area of the City. She was just seventeen but instead of studying at school last term for her A-levels, he'd taught her to open locks, tricks to improve night vision, how to swivel through small spaces and tread lightly. *He'd* put on too much weight during that last stretch inside. He said she'd have to do it for him from now on, or else Mum……..! And that line was never finished. Her imagination created worse terrors than his words ever could. This was her fourth time breaking in somewhere, and she was so so sorry but what else could she do! She was scared of him, but her Mum was terrified.

As he listened, the gun dropped lower and lower. Adrenaline leached away, and by the time the young voice faded out, he too felt slumped. This poor child was no dangerous intruder, no threat to him. What was he to do?

Later that night…

The last Police Car had left. The kitchen sink was full of empty cups. The air was still quivering from sharp-shot questions, hesitant answers, accusations, affirmations, promises and at last, finally, now the hint of returning peace. A second tale had been told, this time mostly fictional. Of a couple meeting randomly on a park bench and of a nerve-taut teenager unexpectedly breaking down at the kindness of an offered sandwich. The same family background had been described truthfully, but the rest of this tale had been devised by the ex-Military man who all his life had fought against the abuse of power. It had not been disclosed that a second burglary of his house had been planned by the Colonel himself and the young girl, secreting compromising evidence to incriminate her brother. Suggestions had however been made to the Police to check here, here and of course there…and don't forget the name of his accomplice in the Town Hall!

The Colonel sat on the same chair in the hall where the first tale had been disclosed. He was exhausted but had one more task to do that long long night. An Uber had been dispatched to fetch Mum. He was waiting to welcome her to stay for a while at his home while her daughter was being questioned, and her situation assessed. Then they could both stay until her son was charged. His lawyer had reassured them that, considering the circumstances and the level of duress employed, any charges for the first three burglaries would be severely mitigated if the Colonel would stand up for such an under-age defendant. Of course he would, without question.

As he waited he mused. It was twenty years ago today. Twenty years since Edith had died. Twenty years in a nowhere land without a wife or children. They'd never been blest with a family. But strangely he felt blest now. His barricades had been smashed, and his future held more such invasions, but for the first time in years, he looked forward to waking up tomorrow.

Footnote:- *Written in response to Paul McCartney's Set at Glastonbury Festival, 25th June 2022. There are five words, phrases or lines from Beatles lyrics in the piece.*

North Coast Writers

Printed in Great Britain
by Amazon

19409482R00139